D1351076

A Gentleman Abroad

Francis Brennan's Travel Tales

GILL BOOKS

Gill Books
Hume Avenue
Park West
Dublin 12
www.gillbooks.ie

Gill Books is an imprint of M.H. Gill and Co.

978 07171 8134 6

Designed by Fidelma Slattery
Edited by Alison Walsh
Copy-edited by Esther Ní Dhonnacha
Printed by ScandBook AB, Sweden

This book is typeset in Linux Libertine and Saint Agnes.

The paper used in this book comes from the wood pulp of managed forests. For every tree felled, at least one tree is planted, thereby renewing natural resources.

A CIP catalogue record for this book is available from the British Library.

5 4 3 2 1

CONTENTS

INTRODUCTION

When I was giving some thought to the subject of travelling for this book, I came across a quote by a Moroccan traveller, Ibn Battuta: 'Travelling: it leaves you speechless, then turns you into a storyteller.' I can't say that I've ever been left speechless by anything, but I understand what he means. I have often been in awe of all the wonderful things I've seen: the bustling cities, the strange and wonderful wildlife, the beautiful monuments, the fantastic scenery and, most of all, the people I've met along the way. And, being a bit of a storyteller, I thought I'd commit my travels to paper and share these journeys with you. Not because I want to show off, but because I hope they'll provide you with a little bit of escapism on a rainy winter's afternoon, and perhaps even a bit of extra knowledge or a travel tip or two.

Unlike Ibn Battuta, who was a 14th-century scholar and who travelled all over the world on a sort of pilgrimage, to understand more about himself and about the places he visited, I'm not a pilgrim: I've never walked the Camino de Santiago, sadly, because I have a wonky foot, and I haven't spent a full 29 years on the road like our Moroccan friend! Nonetheless, I have been fortunate enough in my life to travel a great deal and writing this book has prompted me to reflect a bit on my passion for travel and why I love it so much.

I was lucky enough to begin when travelling was still a glamorous thing: in the days before package travel, getting from A to B was generally long and expensive and while cheap air fares have opened up the world to everyone, which is a good thing, part of me misses the era when people dressed up to the nines to go on a flight – remember that? No tracksuits and Nikes in those days! I can still remember my first trip abroad, with my sister Kate to the wedding of the brother of our French student Claire. Firstly, the very idea of two teens from Balally jetting off to Paris was unheard of, so we were the envy of the neighbourhood, but not only that, the wedding was out of this world. Kate and I spent the trip with our eyes out on stalks admiring the wealthy French, with their gorgeous clothes and sophistication. The wedding was straight from the pages of a celebrity magazine, and afterwards we took in the sights of the city, from the Eiffel Tower to Montmartre to the Jardin des Tuileries. It was absolutely magical. What an introduction to travel – I think it spoiled me! However, I'm mindful of a quote I once read from Paulo Coelho: 'Travel is never a matter of money but of courage.' Absolutely true. The best experiences I've had have been the most unexpected, from a visit to a Maasai home to a holiday chaperoning my 11 nieces and nephews in a minibus that we all remember and talk about to this day. Holidays are about the experiences, but also about the memories.

It hasn't always been glamour, of course: every year I spend seven weeks in the United States, lugging big boxes of travel brochures around from city to city, taking an endless succession of flights (poor you, Francis, I hear you say!) as part of my Tourism Ireland job. It's hard work and between flying in to a new city, setting up our 'show', working hard to woo Americans to Ireland, then packing everything away and flying off to the next destination, there's not much time to wander around to take in the sights, but when there is, I drink it all in. I have become an expert at getting an early flight to my destination so that I can have a wander, or making sure that if we have a rare night off, we have booked tickets for a show or some kind of tourist experience. I'm a sucker for hop-on, hop-off buses (the best way to see a place quickly) and for finding one-off trips for my travelling companions. I love organising things, as those of you who have seen my *Grand Tour* will probably know, but I don't do it for 'celebrity' reasons, even though I've loved making the show and meeting the lovely people who have come with me. I actually first started organising trips for my pals in Skål, the professional travel organisation, and discovered that I liked it, because I enjoy making other people happy. It's a role that I find natural; I'm not a drinker, so I'm always up and about early and chivvying the rest onto the bus, and I get such a buzz from giving my travelling companions an unforgettable experience.

I have been keeping a diary of my travels since 1966 and I have enjoyed leafing through them immensely when researching this book; they bring back such happy memories. I treasure them and the people I've met along the way. In this book, you'll learn quite a bit about me by the places I've visited, the foods I've eaten and the friends I've made, as well as the weird and wonderful things that have happened to me on my travels. You'll find out things about me that might surprise you, and isn't that great? That's what travel is all about – finding out things about yourself that you might not expect. Maybe you'll have discovered that you hate spicy food or that heat brings you out in a rash, but perhaps you'll also discover that you are braver than you thought you were, or more adventurous; that eating foreign foods and talking to people who don't share your language is fun and exciting. Finding out about other cultures really does broaden the mind.

However, the thing about travel is that we always come home. In my case, I love every moment of my journeys, but when I open the hall door of my home in Co. Kerry, put down my suitcases and go into the kitchen to put the kettle on, I feel a real sense of homecoming. I sit on the sofa in the living room with a cup of tea, taking in the garden, forgetting about the big pile of post on the hall table, just having a moment before plunging back into the day-to-day realities of work and business. One of my friends calls it 'reentry', as if I'm coming back from outer space! It really does feel like that sometimes, and I admit that there can be a fair amount of moaning and groaning, but just for those few minutes, as I sit there listening to the birds and the rain falling on the window, I know that I'm home. There really is nothing like it.

Happy travelling!

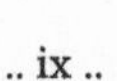

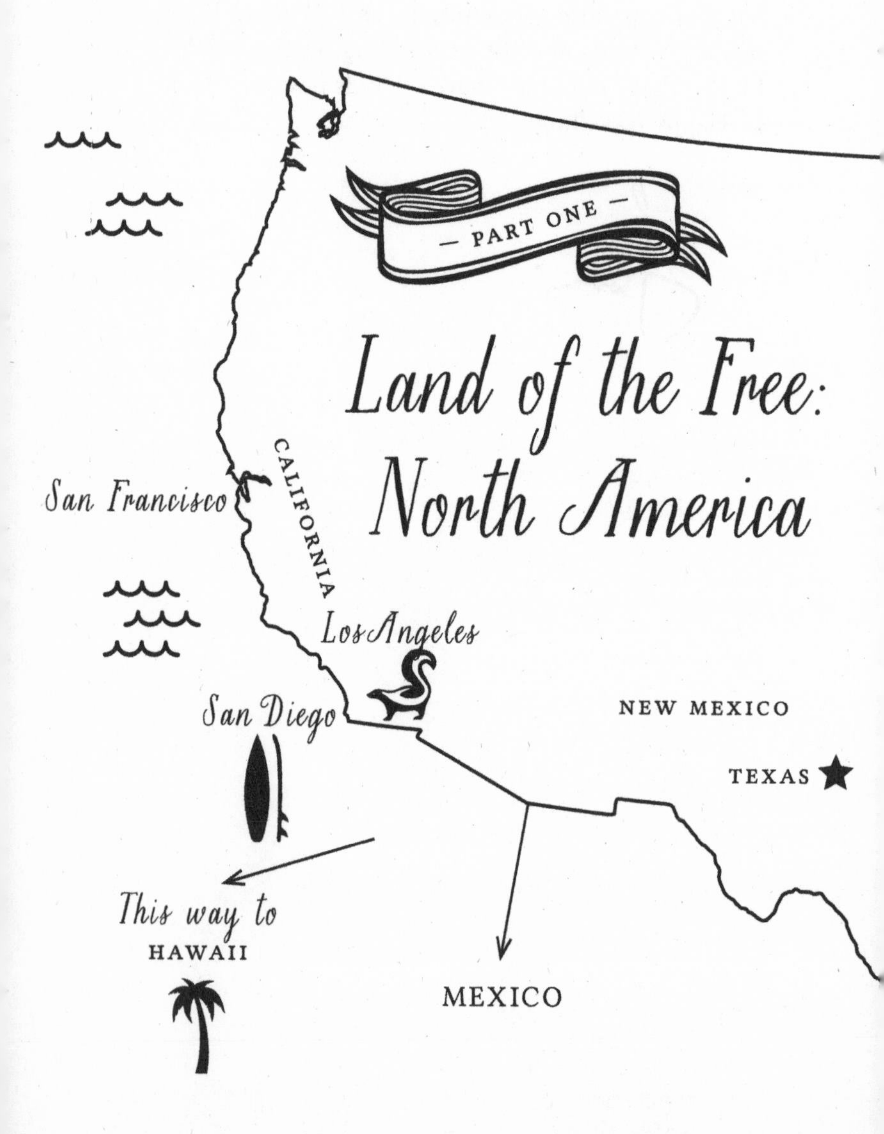
— PART ONE —
Land of the Free:
North America
CALIFORNIA
San Francisco
Los Angeles
San Diego
NEW MEXICO
TEXAS
This way to
HAWAII
MEXICO

N
W
E
S
CANADA
Boston
New York
PENNSYLVANIA
Chicago
St Louis
Dallas
Houston
FLORIDA
Orlando
Miami

'In the unlikely story that is America, there has never been anything false about hope.' –

Barack Obama

When the Beatles were touring America in 1964, a reporter asked Ringo Starr, 'How do you find America?' He replied, 'Turn left at Greenland.' This joke has always amused me, because of course the reporter wanted to know what he thought about the place! America has a special place in my heart. Some people say that it has changed, but in my experience it remains the country I have always loved. I love the people, their friendliness and warmth; I love the big cities and the can-do attitude and the scale of everything. In America, nothing is impossible, and because

I spend seven weeks of every year there, it's a country I've come to know very well, criss-crossing it every springtime for Tourism Ireland, often taking in as many as 40 cities in one trip. But the irony is, unlike practically everyone else, I never got to emigrate there – nearly, but not quite. And do you know what? I'm happy now that I didn't.

When I was in college in the 1970s, along with all my friends, I wanted to get to America. The perception was that if you got there, you were made. So, when I left Dublin College of Catering in 1978, my first job was in Parknasilla in Sneem, Co. Kerry. Lo and behold, Mr Edwards, CEO of Hilton Hotels in America, came to stay – I couldn't believe my luck. I made it my goal to approach him and ask him about going to the States – this was my once-in-a-lifetime opportunity, or so I thought, so I waited for the right moment and delivered my little speech. 'I'm a newly graduated student from catering college and I'd love the opportunity to work in America.' He was very nice and clearly well used to being asked, so he offered me his card. 'When you get settled, send me your CV and I'll get it into the right channels and we'll talk to you.' I was delighted with myself, and sent off my CV, watching the post like a hawk for any reply.

As it happened, Hilton Hotels were opening a pub called Kitty O'Shea's in the Palmer House Hotel in Chicago. Some of you might know the Palmer House as it's a real landmark in Chicago, a real old-fashioned swanky hotel from the time when that kind of opulence was all the rage: 20 floors high, with seven ballrooms and swimming pools and fabulous decor – chandeliers, thick carpets, the lot. You can imagine my excitement. The man in charge of the new pub was the Hilton's food and beverage manager, Benny Martin from Sligo, and the first I knew that Mr Edwards had been as good as his word was when I got a letter one January morning from Benny. He said he'd like to interview me for a position at Kitty O'Shea's and, by the way, was my mother Maura Gallagher from Sligo? Clearly, the Irish network was going strong in Chicago, because there was nothing on my CV mentioning Sligo!

The next time I was home, I said to my mother, 'Do you know Benny Martin?' and she said, 'Oh, of course I do. I went out with him once. He took me on a bike to a dance in Ballintubber.' The penny dropped. Only in Ireland! It turned out that Benny was from Mum's native county and she also told me that his brother used to make suits for Frank Sinatra, which impressed me no end. Benny had ended up in America and had gone on to great things at the Hilton.

I've always had luck like that, I think. Just when I'm least expecting it, something good happens, and I was delighted with myself when Benny said he'd progress my application for a work visa through the American embassy. I was well and truly on my way, I thought. However, my usual good luck seemed to have run out, because it was the year of the postal strike, which lasted from January to May, and what's more, the P&T, as they were called then, ran the telephone system as well – so we couldn't make or receive calls. It probably seems unreal in this day and age, but for five long months, there was no communication at all from or to Parknasilla. (You might well ask how we managed to run a business, but they were different times!) So I heard nothing further from Benny until May, when the strike was over and an avalanche of post arrived at the hotel. One of the letters was from the Hilton, of course, and in it, Benny Martin wrote to tell me to present myself at the American embassy in Ballsbridge on 11 February – three months earlier – to process my Green Card. It was too late, and when I rang the embassy, the nice people told me to forget it. I never did get to America, at least, not in the way I'd intended. Life is like that, full of unexpected forks in the road, and just when you think you're headed one way, you veer off down another path. If I'd gone to America to work for Benny, who knows where I'd be now or what I'd be doing?

Now, I love my trips to America every spring and even though it's hard work, with all those flights and tourism shows, I feel fortunate. I've met so many people and made so many memories over the years, and even though the shows are different these days, and there isn't such a big gang of us on the road (at one stage, there used to be 40 of us travelling together, but now, we're about a dozen), I still love what I do, telling Americans all about Ireland and encouraging them to visit.

The Lone Star State

Sometimes, I'm amused at the kind of customer I get, such as the lady who approached me at a trade show in Dallas, Texas. Now, I have to tell you that Dallas is a great city. Until I came to know it, I thought that it was all the Ewings and Southfork from the TV show of the same name (and yes, you can do a tour of the ranch!), and there certainly is no shortage of 'bling', but in spite of its futuristic skyline, it's unpretentious, bustling, with great food and great culture. I love the Botanical Gardens, particularly in springtime, when they have the most fantastic displays of spring flowers and cherry blossom, and in autumn, when the trees in the arboretum are ablaze. They have wonderful classical music if that's your thing, and there's a museum of Asian art called the Crow Collection of Asian Art, which is spectacular, and, of course, the Sixth Floor Museum overlooking Dealey Plaza, which you may recognise as the famous Texas School Book Depository, where Lee Harvey Oswald took aim on JFK's motorcade. And, as you'll see shortly, there is quite a lot of cowboy entertainment, as you'd expect.

Anyway, there I was at the trade show in Dallas when a lady came up to me and said that she'd never been to Ireland and would love to go. I outlined various areas of interest in the country and told her how many visitors came to Kerry every year. She looked interested and asked me how she'd get to Kerry from Dallas. I said she could fly from Dallas to Chicago or New York, then on to Dublin or to Shannon.

'How far are you from Dublin?' she asked.

I said, 'Four hours.'

'Four *hours*?' she said in astonishment. 'Oh, no, my husband wouldn't stay in a car for four hours.'

Well, I thought, you're some spoiled Dallas queen, but I was being very nice, as these events teach you great patience. 'Well,' I said, 'If you fly to Shannon, it's only two and a half hours from there to Kenmare.'

'Oh, no,' she insisted. 'He'd never stand for that.' Oh, God, I thought, and then she said, 'Is there no other way we could get there?'

I racked my brains, then said, 'Well, you could fly to London and then London to Cork and then we're only an hour and a quarter away. Would he do that?'

'He might,' she replied, 'but why would we fly to London?'

'Well,' I said, mystified, 'you'd save time – you said you didn't want to do four hours from Dublin.'

'It's an awfully long way around the world,' she replied.

Well, I thought, I'm sorry they put Kerry so far away from you, but needless to say, I didn't tell her that out loud. 'Inside thoughts', a friend of mine calls them! 'Well, it's the only way of getting to us,' I replied.

'Have you not got an airport near you?' she said. 'You see, we have our own plane.'

Sacred Heart, I thought. 'Well, you never said. That's marvellous! Oh, sure, everyone has one of them – what's the fuss?' I went on to say she could fly it to Farranfore, only 28 miles from Kenmare and a very well-equipped airport too. 'I think it can take a 747,' I added helpfully.

'Oh,' she said, 'we don't have one of them.' I felt like saying, 'How very disappointing.' She probably had a Learjet. Everything in Dallas is bigger and better. She never did come for a visit!

I also have very fond memories of the Stockyards in Fort Worth, a city that's actually 30 miles away from

Dallas, but is within what's called the DFW metroplex, that is, the greater area of Dallas–Fort Worth–Arlington. Fort Worth is sometimes known as Cowtown, for a reason, because it's the home of the rodeo, and indeed its flag has a steer on it. It also has a world-class gallery, the Kimbell Art Museum, which actually does look like a cattle shed – which is not an insult, but entirely fitting given the location, and it's lovely, with a stunning collection. Anyway, on this particular visit in 1986, I was coming into Fort Worth with Bord Fáilte, as it was known at the time, for work. As we had so little free time – we'd always be working very hard all day, then pack up our road show and go to the airport and fly out – often the only spare hours would be the night before a show, if we were lucky enough to get in in the afternoon. I'm always on the lookout for shows that might be on in the places we're visiting, and in Fort Worth, I hit pay dirt! That very night, the rodeo was on, and as I'd never seen one, I thought it would be great. An American friend of mine, Cilla, got six tickets, two for herself and her husband and four for the Irish gang, and off we went.

The Stockyards in Fort Worth are like an Irish mart, only on a giant scale: they were where they used to bring all the cattle, and all the breeders would come to buy them, going back to the 1920s. The show was just fantastic, with lots of bullriding, lassoing and other cowboy activities, and the place was jam-packed with people, like All-Ireland Day here. There was a place where you could get your hat steamed to get it nice and clean, and competitions for the best-dressed cowboy and cowgirl. After all that excitement, we retired to a giant Texan bar, which had a huge dancefloor with a pole in the middle – not that kind of pole! – and you had to dance around it in a circle. If you went the wrong way, you'd be killed. The band were brilliant and we had a blast. Then I spotted that they had a mechanised rodeo bull, which impressed me no end. We'd never seen the like of it in Ireland, but I wasn't going to be foolish enough to get on it. My friend Majella was with me – a great girl – and nothing would do me but to get her up on the bull. Eventually, she decided she'd have a go. She hung on, but only lasted about 20 seconds, which is not bad! To this day, she always says, 'I'll never forget when you got me on the bull in Fort Worth.'

Whenever I travel, I always get the cheapest flight, because I like to do things at the right price, but sometimes I like to treat myself and I'll go to the Rosewood Mansion on Turtle Creek, which, for me, is the nicest hotel in Dallas. It's gorgeous, with its golden stone and turrets and towers – not authentic, of course; nothing in Dallas is 'old' in the sense that we know it – but built in the 1920s. The original owners travelled Europe in search of inspiration, lucky them, and apparently the architecture is Renaissance in inspiration. It's certainly lovely and elegant, and one of my absolute favourite places to stay. Mind you, when I was staying there for a show once, I did get nabbed by a very elegantly dressed man who mistook me for a wealthy Dallas citizen and invited me to the launch of a floating apartment cruise ship called the Residensea. Can you imagine? An apartment on this ship costs an initial €3 million plus an annual €400k service charge, and you can go all over the world on it – you can go to Rio for the Carnival ... the lady with the private jet probably bought one! The man gave me a lot of bumf about it and they kept sending it to me for years, not that I was tempted! I've never even been on board, sadly, but my brother John was a guest at a lunch on board and says it's out of this world.

New Mexico is next door to Texas; sadly, I haven't spent much time there, although I did send one of my chefs in the Park Hotel Kenmare there some years ago, which provided me with a nice story. We usually send the staff off to other hotels in the closed season to improve their education and to bring home ideas from other parts of the world. I said to my chef at the time, Bruno, 'Where would you like to go?' He said he'd love to get experience of cooking 'new American cuisine'. What he meant by that was the new, lighter style of cooking that was taking shape in places like California and New Mexico, with lots of bright flavours. Now, I knew a Mrs Stevens, who owned a hotel in Santa Fe, New Mexico, so I said I'd set him up with a stage, as we call it, with her.

It all worked out very well, but about a week before he was due to go, he came into the office and said, 'I'm just wondering what to bring her as a gift.'

I said, 'How about an Aran jumper? It'll never go out of style and will be very acceptable.'

'Great idea!' he said, and went off into Kenmare to get a nice one for Mrs Stevens.

Now, this was long before you could look places up like you can nowadays and we probably didn't have many guidebooks on New Mexico at the time, so Bruno had imagined that a hot desert would be waiting for him. A week or so later, off he flew, expecting to be hit with a wall of sunshine on his arrival. He got the fright of his life, because it was under two feet of snow! New Mexico is at a very high altitude and snow in the winter is not at all uncommon, but poor Bruno wasn't prepared. He had a suitcase full of shorts, T-shirts and runners, and so frozen was he, he didn't part with the Aran sweater, but wore it himself!

I remember that he came back with all kinds of fresh ideas from New Mexico, like guacamole and chilli sauces, and a lovely corn soup. I hadn't realised that New Mexican food is a bit different. It's not Mexican, I'm told, and it's not Tex-Mex either, which uses a lot of beef and cheese. There are elements of both in it, but it has a style all of its own. McDonald's in New Mexico even has a green chilli burger! Green chilli is a cornerstone of New Mexican cooking and apparently at holiday time, green chilli stew is served everywhere. It reminds me a little bit of Irish stew, except that it uses beef or pork and a ton of green chilli! They even have a special chilli festival in the autumn to celebrate their favourite spicy vegetable. Sopapillas are another must-eat in New Mexico, little flaky pastry parcels that can be filled with mince for savoury eating, or cheese or, yes, chilli! But it can also be sweet, with a little honey drizzled over it.

You Can't Take Them Anywhere

Returning to my brother John, some of my fondest memories of the States involve him, and indeed travelling with Mum, which I've done twice, and also, unforgettably, with my 11 nieces and nephews. I'm sure John didn't enjoy the first story I'm about to tell you, but we can laugh about it now. And it's set in one of my favourite parts of the country, California. I haven't spent quite as much time as I'd like in the Golden State, as it's usually been all about the work, but I have come to know Los Angeles reasonably well, even though its charms are not obvious at first! Some people love that year-long blue sky and sunshine, and yes, it's great to get a dose of it in early spring, when it's cold and grey back in Kerry, but I find the smog and the traffic hard work.

I prefer to take the Pacific Coast Highway up to San Francisco, or down to San Diego. You'll probably have heard of this road, as it's one of the great scenic routes of the world and it is spectacular – twisting and turning high up above the Pacific Ocean, under that gorgeous blue sky, made famous by Clint Eastwood's *Play Misty for Me.* There's Big Sur, with the huge mountains that slope down to the ocean. There's the breathtaking Hearst Castle in San Simeon, a huge estate built by William Randolph Hearst for his art collection, and home to magnificent rooms and gardens. The lovely Pfeiffer Beach is an absolute must at sunset: there's a rock formation, Keyhole Arch, through which you can peek at the setting sun. And it has purple sand! Apparently, the colour is due to minerals that wash down from the mountains. Now, American beaches are not like Irish beaches – they have entrance fees (I know!) and opening and closing times, which might not please those of us keen on our evening bonfires and barbecues, but America is more regimented than here, I find, a bit more organised, which has its good and bad points.

Carmel is another lovely spot on the Pacific Coast Highway, with another pristine beach, this time with golden sand. It's probably most famous for its one-time mayor Clint Eastwood, but it was originally a Spanish mission and an artists' retreat. In many ways, it resembles a cute English country village. This is due to the presence of a number of Comstock cottages, fairy-tale little houses with shingle roofs, timber frames, ornate windows and gorgeous little wrought-iron door knockers and bells. They were built in the 1920s by a Mr Hugh Comstock, initially for his wife who wanted a house for her doll collection, but then he got carried away and filled the town with them! You can take a guided tour to learn more about them, or if you wander around, you'll keep coming across them. The gardens, with their brick patios and rambling roses, are a favourite of mine. The cottages give Carmel a unique, antique atmosphere that really is like nowhere else in America.

Anyway, back to poor John, who never got anywhere near the Comstock cottages, for reasons that will become clear. When I first started to do the shows in the USA, John was working in the Sligo Park Hotel and hadn't yet gone to America. He felt positively left out, as you can imagine, so when Tourism Ireland wanted help and hands to lug boxes from place to place, my good friend Jean said, 'Would John like to come out?' He was only delighted to take holidays from work and come along.

We worked through New York and Chicago and John was thrilled with it all, particularly seeing the Big Apple for the first time. However, when he got to LA, he wasn't feeling well, and next thing, he was covered in red spots. It turned out he had chicken pox and, as he was an adult, he got it really badly. The doctor came to see him in his hotel room and told him he'd have to be quarantined for at least ten days, and poor John was devastated. But when the good doctor asked him if he was with a group, he had the presence of mind to say no, because otherwise all 40 of us would have had to be quarantined!

So, John had to stay in the hotel while the rest of us went on to Tampa in Florida. I can remember that he wasn't happy about that. We were staying in the Century Plaza in Los Angeles as I remember, with the staff leaving his food outside the door. It was a really nice hotel, a gigantic 19-storey modern building shaped in a crescent – pure modern America, but I think it was slightly lost on John. One bright spot was that, at the time, the actor Telly Savalas lived in the hotel. He was very famous because he'd played Kojak, the lollipop-sucking detective, and was a big star. When he found out there was an Irish fellow there, he used to come to John's room every day for a chat – isn't that nice? Presumably he was immune to chicken pox!

When I mentioned to John that the chicken pox story would feature in my new book, he reminded me of a little coda to it that I'd forgotten. After his quarantine, he followed the group to Boston, the next town on our agenda, shuffling onto the flight in his T-shirt, jeans and runners and the big coat he'd bought for colder destinations. When he got to the Boston Park Plaza, face covered in red spots, with calamine lotion all over him, in his scruffy attire, he was surprised to find the staff making an enormous fuss of him. 'Mr Brennan, you're in the Garden Room,' the receptionist told him. Very nice, he thought, even if, when he got upstairs, it didn't seem to be all that exciting, just a pleasant hotel room with a view of the hotel gardens. Anyway, John settled in and went downstairs to start getting the conference room ready for the show and to meet the rest of the gang after his enforced isolation, and when he got back up to his room later, there was a lady sitting outside it on a chair. 'I'm terribly sorry, Mr Brennan,' she said, 'I've been off duty since nine a.m., but I made an awful mistake. You were meant to be in the Garden Suite, so I've taken the liberty of moving your baggage. I hope you don't mind.' John wasn't delighted, because I had given him a nice belt as a present that got lost in the move, but he allowed himself to be shown to his new room, which was a three-bed suite with a dining-room table set for 14 people, a baby grand piano, a big sitting room and a fireplace! John was thrilled, if a bit puzzled – he wasn't expecting 14 guests. It transpired that when the reservations manager had seen the name 'John Brennan' on the list, he'd convinced himself that it was actually Seamus Brennan, the then minister for tourism. 'I was the one with the runners and the jeans and the beard a week old, face covered in spots – and they thought I was a government minister.'

There's always a lot of excitement around John Brennan, as I remember well from that tour. Before the chicken pox incident, John and I had worked our way down to San Diego, south of Los Angeles. It's not far from the Mexican border, so it has a really Spanish feel to it, but it also has a tree-lined Victorian centre, and it's perfect for browsing in the shops, walking along the palm-lined beaches and cycling in the parks. It is so laid back. In truth, John and I weren't taking in too much of the scenery during this visit because we were busy, but one incident really sticks in both our minds.

We were staying in a hotel complex in downtown San Diego and, at the time, there were ferocious thunderstorms (we tend to forget that California isn't all sea and sunshine). John was sitting out on the balcony of our room, and during a particularly heavy downpour, he noticed that there was water flooding everywhere. 'C'mon, we'll go downstairs and have a look,' he said. Then, to my alarm, we heard a sudden firecracker sound, which we both knew to be gunshots, and he got even more excited – he was a young man at this stage and Sligo wasn't gunshot alley – but as his sensible older brother, I was reluctant to set foot outside the room. Eventually, he looked out another window and noticed that the street was filling with water. 'Oh, come on, Francis, let's go down and have a look.'

'All right then,' I said reluctantly, unwilling to let him venture out on his own – if something happened to him, Mum would kill me.

The street that runs along the front of the hotel leads to a bridge, which is designed to open at the sides to let the overflow of water escape. However, with the sheer volume of water, which we could see tumbling down the ravine behind the hotel, suddenly the street was awash. Next thing, from our vantage point on the sidewalk, a Lincoln town car – a big, square American car – came down the street and, in spite of us all yelling at them to stop, ploughed into the water. There were four blue-rinse elderly ladies in it, and to our horror, they drove straight into this lake. As the water rose, the lights of the car began to dim. Because everything in these cars is electric, of course the car was now completely immobile – and they couldn't open the windows either. Thankfully, one of the blue-rinse ladies had had her window open and the next thing we knew, she was clambering out of it to perch on the bonnet, while the car filled with the water, now a raging torrent.

Next thing, the coastguard appeared. Now, we were in the middle of the city of San Diego, so John nearly had hysterics when he saw it: it would be like seeing the RNLI in the middle of O'Connell Street. The coastguard had a surfboard on the roof of his jeep, which John thought was even more funny, with visions of one of the ladies surfing off down the street. So, the coastguard fired a harpoon out to the car that caught in the roof, and then he stretched its rope out and clambered along it to get to the ladies. He got them all out of the car and onto the bonnet and then Coastguard Team Two launched a little inflatable boat and shot another harpoon; my man attached this to the car as well and then put the ladies, one by one, into the boat. There was no shooting, which we'd come to see, but this was ample reward.

On another trip to California, when I was chairman of Small Luxury Hotels of the World (SLHW), we had our congress in La Jolla, which is about 20 kilometres north of San Diego, on the coast. It's idyllic, as you'd expect, with seven miles of beaches and Torrey Pines wildlife reserve, which has all kinds of wildlife, from bobcats to skunks and all kinds of wild birds. It's a very popular place for hikes. Now, I'd got terribly excited about the location and decided that we'd have a party on the beach one night – a barbecue for 400 people, as you do! We had a man from Hawaii make genuine Hawaiian shirts for everyone to wear, but the weather turned out to be absolutely freezing, so at the last minute, I had to go to a local market and bulk buy black hoodies to keep everyone warm. (As a nice little aside, my Hawaiian shirt ended up playing a starring role in a school production of *Joseph and the Amazing Technicolour Dreamcoat*. My good friend Frank used to teach in a secondary school on the north side of Dublin and asked if he could borrow that 'mad shirt' of mine to go under Joseph's coat – I never saw it again.)

That's the thing about California: everyone assumes it's an idyll, but with the forest fires, flash floods and earthquakes it makes Ireland, with its merely variable weather, look quite appealing. I can clearly remember one earthquake in San Francisco in 1994. Again, it was a work trip and we were all staying at the Holiday Inn, Union Square. It's at the heart of the city, with all the big stores, like Macy's and Saks Fifth Avenue on it, and the Westin St Francis Hotel, another one of those big, swanky American hotels. There's a lovely street called Maiden Lane that runs off Union Square that's full of art galleries and restaurants and tables out on the street for people-watching – but apparently, during the Gold Rush, it played host to ladies of the night! Must be where it got its name ...

We stayed up until the early hours talking, as we often did when we were all on the road, and I crawled up to bed at 4 a.m. I thought, I'm exhausted, I'll run a bath and relax in it and then I'll sleep really well, so I got into the bath and lay back: the bathroom had been decorated with foil paper with yachts on it, as I recall, and I think it stuck in my mind because of what happened next. Suddenly, I found myself under the water. I got such a fright, because one minute, I was soaking nicely, the next, my face was four inches under the water. Maybe I'd fallen asleep, I thought, deciding that I'd better get out, because if I fell asleep again, I'd drown. It took me a while to nod off, I can tell you.

The next morning, I saw on the news that there had been an earthquake and when I chatted to the woman at reception, she informed me that anti-earthquake buildings sway, which explained the little tidal wave in my bath. Imagine – to drown in an earthquake on the 20th floor! I was highly amused, however, when one of the gang got onto the *Irish Independent* about 'surviving the earthquake' and got lots of press out of it, while he'd actually slept through the whole thing. If only I'd been quicker off the mark.

I can remember another near miss in a little suburban town in the San Francisco Bay Area, Moraga, where I'd been invited to spend the weekend by the CEO of Transamerica. (Transamerica had started to fly to Ireland, which was big news at the time, as we didn't have Pan Am or United Airlines or any of the big carriers, but it's probably best known for the Transamerica Pyramid, an iconic skyscraper in a triangle shape, wide at the bottom and narrowing to a point at the top. It was once the eighth tallest building in the world, at 853 feet. When you consider that the Burj Khalifa in Dubai is 2,717 feet, that doesn't seem very tall, but in 1972, America led the way for skyscrapers, as well as for everything else.)

The CEO had just had a new house built and invited me to come out to Moraga to stay for the weekend. I knew that the house had cost $850,000, which was a fortune at the time, and I was eager to have a look – it didn't disappoint, being absolutely spectacular. But then, in the middle of the night, I was awoken by a loud banging on the bedroom door and shouts of 'Get up, get up, quick!' I jumped up, threw on the robe I'd been given and my slippers and ran outside. It was pouring from the heavens at this point and we and the neighbours who lived in the four other substantial homes in the cul-de-sac stood outside in our pyjamas huddled under umbrellas. It transpired that there had been a small earthquake and in the heavy rain, they were worried that their homes might slide down the hill. I couldn't believe it – I'd prefer to be in my own place at home in Kerry, rather than in this amazing house, which could disappear at any moment! It didn't slide down the hill on that occasion, but to this day I often wonder if the house is still standing – I suppose it's the price you pay if you live somewhere like that, beautiful, but fragile.

In fact, the recent volcano in Hawaii reminded me of how lovely places like this are often not easy to live in and it makes me feel all the more grateful for home. I first visited Hawaii in 1989 with Skål and we were staying in the Sheraton Waikiki Hotel. As you can imagine, it was very much sun and sandy beaches: Waikiki Beach is one of the most famous beaches in the world, a lovely long curve of sand with Diamond Head or Leahi (that's 'brow of the tuna' in the native language) a large green hump in the background. Unlike the north of the island of Oahu, the sea here is relatively calm, but with enough waves for most surfers. In fact, Hawaii's most famous surfer, Duke Kahanamoku, known as the Big Kahuna, learned at Waikiki and there's a statue of him on the seafront. I don't surf, because of my foot, but I do scuba dive, of which more later ...

I used to love to look out at the bay from my hotel balcony after dinner, because the sunsets were fantastic, with all of the beautiful colours, but I was usually in bed fairly early. I don't like to overdo it on holiday and, as a non-drinker, I'm usually up early the next day. One night, I was fast asleep, and the bed moved underneath me. Now, in case you're wondering, these beds were built up from the floor, so they were *very* solid. The bed shook again and I thought, oh no, there's something under my bed. And then it shook again, and my subconscious went into overdrive. It must be an alligator, I thought sleepily – it couldn't be anything else. Quite why I thought this, I have no idea. I suppose my mind was trying to come up with a plausible explanation for the bed shaking.

The floor seemed to be moving underneath me, so I thought it better not to step onto it. Instead, I stood up on the bed and jumped from the bed to the sofa and looked back to see if this alligator was there. By this stage, I'd woken up fully and remembered that I was on the 12th floor, so no alligator could have got up here – unless he took a lift! With my mind now working properly, I figured that it was an earthquake and I remembered being told that the safest place to stand is under the lintel of the door, so I charged out to the balcony and put one foot on it and the other foot in my room. Then it occurred to me that if there was another shake, the balcony might fall off, so I put my foot in. By this stage, the rumbling and shaking had stopped and I wondered if it had all been a dream. It was four o'clock in the morning after all – maybe I just had indigestion. I went into the bathroom to get an antacid and noticed that my hairdryer plug was like a pendulum, swinging back and forth, so I guessed that I'd been right. The next day, we learned that there had been an earthquake on another island and it had done a lot of damage over there, but we had only got shaken. It's funny what the mind will do when it's not quite awake!

Feeling the Fear

John certainly enlivened that particular year's trip to the States, and Mum has kept me company a couple of times now. The first time we travelled together was when I brought Mum to America to see her cousins, the nuns. These relatives were a subject of fascination to me on their one and only visit to Ireland, after many years in America. They were from the Katharine Drexel order, which I'd never heard of before. Katharine Drexel is a saint and only the second American to have been canonised, would you believe, for her work with Native Americans, and indeed the two nuns had taught Native American children in New Orleans. What interested me most were their elaborate and enormous wimples, a large square box shape around their heads. I can still see them, sitting in the back of Mum's old Morris Minor, on the way to Sligo for a shopping trip!

On this particular trip, I remember that after our visit to the nuns, I was working in Florida for a week, but Mum was going up to New York to see a cousin of hers and had to take the flight on her own. She's a bit of a worrier, Mum, and terrified of flying, so I tried to reassure her. 'Now, Mum, I'll see you to the gate. Jean [my friend] will meet you in New York and take you to see Helen [her cousin], so all you have to do is sit on the plane on your own.' At the very mention of the words 'on your own', she began to panic. Mum overthinks things sometimes, so when she got on the plane and found she had a window seat, she panicked even more. When she goes to Mass, she likes to be out at the edge, because if there's a fire, she'll get out first, so on a plane, she always likes the aisle seat, for easy escape!

She took her seat uneasily, thinking, if anyone large sits beside me, I'll never get out of the seat when the crash happens. Catastrophising, I think they call it. Sure enough, a rather big American man came down the plane and Mum's mind began to run away with her, imagining what it might be like to clamber over him in the event of an accident. Of course, he sat down beside her and Mum thought, that's it then – I'll definitely die now when the plane crashes. So, the plane taxied out and rumbled down the runway, Mum gripping the armrest, and as it flew down the runway, the man suddenly leaned over to her and said, 'Excuse me. Can I hold your hand? Because I'm terrified.'

'You're not as terrified as me!' Mum replied cheerfully, offering him her hand. As it happens, they became great friends on the flight, chatting away until they landed in New York.

You'd be surprised just how many people are afraid of flying. I'm not, which is a good job, because I have to do so much of it, but I sympathise with those who are terrified. You always know who they are, because of the sweat pouring from their brows or the nervous shifting in the seat, and I always feel for them. I tell myself that accidents and that kind of thing are outside my control and once I understand that, I can relax. However, I was reminded how painful it can be for some people when I was in Logan Airport in Boston once, trying to get to St Louis, Missouri. I was going to the funeral of an old friend of mine, Shirley, a lovely woman, a travel agent from St Louis, who loved Ireland and sent people to me more than a dozen times over the years.

I had been on Cape Cod for a few days' vacation, and it's a place that I love, because of the mix of old-world American charm and the pretty sandy beaches. It's the seaside, but not as we know it here. On Cape Cod, it's all about lovely villages and seafood shacks and bicycle rides – no damp, sandy sandwiches! When I heard the sad news about Shirley, I booked my flight and drove up to Logan. When I got there, I found that my flight had been cancelled, for reasons that weren't clear – it happens quite a lot – but the airline rep added, 'We've rerouted you over Miami,' giving me a big smile, as if to say, 'Isn't that great news?' For God's sake, I thought, that's like going to Belfast via Kerry.

I asked her if she could put me on standby for the next flight out. 'Well, there are 19 people ahead of you,' she said politely.

'I'll take a gamble,' I said, 'and if I don't get on, I'll go via Miami.'

The next hour was spent at the gate, observing my fellow standby passengers and praying that they would somehow decide not to go. An elderly gentleman came up with his wife and I was watching him like a hawk. The next thing, he went behind the counter at the gate and started tapping. Clearly, he was a former employee, retired, who was putting his name down for the flight. My heart sank. He was bound to be ahead of me in the queue then, I thought.

An hour later, I was in a complete lather, watching the flight being called and everyone getting on and thinking how I'd miss Shirley's funeral. I was still watching my elderly friends and off they went through the gate. The staff were calling and calling and my chances of not going to St Louis via Hong Kong were narrowing by the minute. Finally, I saw them closing the door out to the tarmac and I thought, oh, no, that's it. I went up to the airline lady and said, 'Is that it?'

'Sorry,' she replied. 'I'm just going to re-ticket you via Miami.' Brilliant, I thought, knowing that I'd be in St Louis a day late for Shirley's funeral.

The next thing, the door to the aircraft opened and this lady came charging down the corridor and out through the door to the gate. 'I can't go!' she shouted at the top of her voice. She was in the throes of a panic attack and was bawling crying. The staff were so nice to her and talked to her and tried to encourage her to get back on, while I was looking on thinking, please don't get a second wind. I know, it doesn't sound nice, but I really wanted to get to St Louis. It turned out from the chatter that she was a baker and was heading to some trade show that she'd now miss, but nothing would persuade her to get on, so eventually, I was ushered on. I felt sorry for the poor girl, but not that sorry, as I got to St Louis! Shirley's nieces and nephews come to see me all the time in Kenmare. We still have a connection, which is lovely. In fact, I saw them when I was going through St Louis for my Route 66 trip.

But back to Mum! On our first trip to America together, we'd visited the nuns in their convent in Bensalem, Pennsylvania, home to the shrine of St Katharine Drexel herself, and I'd hired a car to drive back to New York, through the lovely Pennsylvania Dutch countryside. This region is famous as the home of the Amish community, with their horse-drawn carriages and simple way of life. Interestingly, it's also the home of unhealthy food! Hershey's has a big outlet factory in Pennsylvania, as do several crisp and pretzel manufacturers, if that's your thing. It's only a three-hour drive and I'm well used to American freeways, so off we went. Mum was happy as Larry, until we drove down 155th Street and into Harlem, which was fairly downtrodden at the time – indeed, New York was still a pretty violent city in the late '80s, so Mum was sitting beside me, praying we wouldn't get a puncture.

We were going to the Paramount Hotel – which was so chi-chi, they didn't put the name on the outside – because I'd been 'comped' by the owner, who had stayed at the Park. Comping means that we offer a complimentary visit in the expectation that the favour will be returned. We had to go up and down West 46th Street ten times, but eventually found it. The Paramount was one of the early boutique hotels and you couldn't see your nose in the gloomy foyer. In the bedroom, at the bed-head was a large screen-print of Van Gogh, so I could lie there, my head resting on his good ear, and the bathroom was filled with stainless steel – including the bath. It was very modern, indeed, ahead of its time, but you can imagine what my mother made of it. She was very quiet over dinner that night, and after one night's stay, she said, 'Francis, can we move hotel? I don't like it here and I'd like to stay in a real hotel.' I knew what she meant! We'd spoiled her with the Park and even though the Paramount was 'hip', it wasn't for her. We checked out and went to the Marriott Marquis, which was a 'real hotel' of the kind that she was used to, with nice, thick carpets, big beds with headboards, bathrooms with white furniture and fluffy towels, and she was very happy.

New York has become something of a second home to me. Somebody asked me recently how many times I've been there and, at a guess, I'd say 60 or 70. I've been going there roughly twice a year for 38 years, so, you do the math, as they say! Having said that it's a second home, I absolutely would not like to live there as the level of energy you'd need is so high. I'd be exhausted at the pace of life and because so many things are a challenge there – transport, accommodation, even moving around – with the result that New Yorkers have an impatience that is understandable, but hard to live with.

The other thing is that in New York, madness is never far away. Just on my most recent visit, I went in search of a diner for breakfast. I always try to hunt down a real diner, because they generally do great breakfasts and, also, you feel you're in the thick of it. I located the Galaxy Diner on 9th Avenue, and was shown to a booth, where I ordered my breakfast. While I was waiting, I did a bit of a Maeve Binchy on it and tuned in to the conversations going on around me. In the booth to my left were two women in their late twenties, having breakfast, or rather, they weren't, because they were too busy bawling their eyes out. Both of them were hysterical and as I tuned in, I discovered that they were talking about their love lives, tears pouring down their faces, breakfasts untouched. To my right, a lady in her sixties sat by herself, tucking in to her breakfast and carrying on an imaginary conversation with someone, who, on closer listening, turned out to be the comedian Carol Burnett, of *The Carol Burnett Show*, among others. I suppose if you want to pick an imaginary dining companion, you could do worse! Anyway, this woman's conversation became more and more animated and louder and louder, until the waiter went over to her and said, 'Now, Anita, could you keep the volume down?'

'Oh, yes!' she replied brightly, her voice a whisper, before the volume started increasing again. That's New York, I always think. You'll never be on your own! There's a whole level of manic madness to the place that works perfectly.

However, if you are simply looking to have a nice time, New York will certainly deliver. Christmas is my favourite time of year in the city. Once, I took my friend Jean's two children to the Holiday Train Show at the New York Botanical Garden, and I enjoyed the spectacle more than they did. The staff recreate some of the city's most iconic structures out of natural materials in the gardens and the little trains whizz in and out of the Brooklyn Bridge and Grand Central Station and lots of other places – it's just magical. I also love the skating rink at Rockefeller Center – I've dreamed about ice skating but never have, because of my foot, but I still used to love to take Jean's two there when they were children – they are adults now, and how quickly time flies. The skating rink is particularly lovely in the evening, when the lights of New York are twinkling and everyone is out on the ice. My third favourite Christmas thing in New York is the Saks Fifth Avenue window displays – or rather, whole-building displays. Every Christmas they mount a gigantic light show on the front of the building, complete with sound effects and fireworks – spectacular and entirely free!

The Magic City

I have to say that Mum doesn't really trust me when it comes to freebies. I'm not bothered by them at all – I'm well used to availing of tickets and deals, and indeed offering them to others. It's what we do in my business, but Mum has never been comfortable with them. She was brought up to take only what she'd paid for and is suspicious of anything else. So, when I offered her the chance to see Julio Iglesias in Miami, she was initially thrilled, but suspicion quickly followed! I was in Miami for the ASTA (American Society of Travel Agents) conference and having a ball. Miami is a fantastic city and I love the ice-cream-coloured Art Deco buildings on South Beach. It's an ideal place to watch the beautiful people – even the dogs are gorgeous in South Beach! If you're in search of something more authentic, Little Havana is a real experience. A predominantly Cuban neighbourhood, it's full of music and bustle and old men playing dominoes, as well as bakeries, delis and restaurants serving Cuban delicacies. Coral Gables is another lovely spot near Miami, with its tree-lined boulevards and open-air Venetian swimming pool, designed by a man with the fantastic name of Phineas Paist and built in 1924 to look like a

Venetian palazzo, with grottos, waterfalls and the like. Of course, there's also the iconic Biltmore Hotel, a vast expanse of pink-painted brick, with a giant bell tower in the middle. It has featured in many a movie and TV show and indeed it's a hotel Mum would approve of.

Prior to every ASTA conference, a headline concert is announced and, on this occasion, Julio Iglesias, who was at the height of his popularity at the time, was to perform. Now, there would be 6,000 delegates at the conference as a rule, but only 2,000 tickets for the concert, so there was usually a big scramble for them. Jean worked for Bord Fáilte and had been given tickets by the CEO, Niall Miller, who wasn't going, so her four tickets became our four tickets. Mum was absolutely delighted, because she loved Julio and because the occasion is high on glamour, with red carpets and fancy lights and style and two big searchlights going up in the air. Off we went in our taxi and when we arrived, Mum got out first, and was faced with a PR girl with a clipboard. 'What names?' she asked.

'Brennan,' my mother said.

I was helping Jean out of the taxi and I corrected her. 'Miller,' I offered to the girl with the clipboard.

'No, Maura Brennan,' my mother insisted, looking at me as if I was mad.

The girl looked up and down the list. 'There's no Brennan here.'

'Mum, it's Miller,' I insisted.

She looked at me. 'Are you at it again, sneaking in under someone else's name? We'll be thrown out.'

I said to the girl, 'Mum's name is Brennan, but it's Miller.'

'Oh, yes,' she said, 'party of four.' Mum gave me the look I deserved, but she loved the concert, so she forgave me in the end. And who wouldn't love a week in Miami?

My favourite memory of Miami is from my stay at the iconic Fontainebleau Hotel on Miami Beach. You might well know this landmark building from shows such as *Miami Vice* and films such as *Goldfinger* and *Scarface*: it's an enormous curved expanse, built in 1954 by a famous modernist architect called Morris Lapidus, with a front lobby that is 17,000 square feet, and gardens modelled on those in the Palace of Versailles – only bigger and better! It truly represented all that was glamorous about Miami in the 1960s and everyone, from Elvis Presley to Judy Garland, hung out there at one point. It's been done up now and is out of this world, but when I stayed in 1984, it was really a case of decaying grandeur – a bit frayed around the edges.

Anyway, during my stay, I was told that there was a huge function to take place on the penthouse floor of the hotel and, being me, I was dying to have a look. I knew that if I took the elevator to the top floor, I'd be turned away, so I took it to one floor below, then hopped up on the fire escape to the top floor. And was I glad I had! They were getting the party ready and my eyes were out on stalks as they laid the tables, with their black tablecloths, gold place settings and elaborate centrepieces; they were installing a whole false ceiling, complete with star constellations, and constructing a circus ring to complete the Cirque du Soleil theme – all this for a 13-year-old's bar mitzvah, as I found out. When I got chatting to the girl in reception later, she informed me that it cost $120,000 – in 1984!

My favourite family trip of all time, though, was the one I took with my 11 nieces and nephews to Florida for ten days. By myself. I don't know what came over me, but I got a notion that I'd like to take them all and even though it was 13 years ago now, they all still talk about it. I suppose that's the thing about family holidays: they're about shared experiences and memories, and with Uncle Francis, they have someone who takes an interest in them, but who isn't their parents, which is a good thing. Their parents thought I was mad, but as the eldest of the children was around 14 or 15 at the time and the youngest was six, I figured that the older ones could look after the younger ones, and they did, and it was a fantastic holiday. Not that they'll thank me for one of these stories, but it's too good not to tell!

We were going to Orlando, a paradise for children – as I often say, all you need is money in Orlando. It eats it, especially if you have a party of 11, but that's what I'd bought into, so off we went. I'd researched all the ways and means of getting around when there and eventually I decided on a 15-seater minibus, which I would drive. We were staying at the Orlando World Center Marriott, a huge resort with pools and rides and endless games and ice-cream, all sorts of things to enchant a child. We took outings to water parks and to Walt Disney World, of course, and did all of the touristy things, but it turned out that one or two of the kids had other ideas.

Outside all of the petrol stations over there, they have those clear plastic bins where you can pick up your *USA Today* and *New York Times.* But, as I discovered, you can also get the kinds of magazines that are of interest to a 15-year-old boy – 'Dial 1800 and she comes to your room' – that kind of thing, if you know what I mean. I knew that there was a certain amount of plotting going on, because I could hear whispering behind me whenever I pulled into a petrol station, and sure enough, one day I went into the shop to pay for my petrol and as I was coming out, I saw one of my nephews running towards one of the containers, grabbing a magazine, then running back towards the minivan and jumping in.

Of course, when I got in, there was a silence as never before. I put my seatbelt on and I looked in the mirror and they were all giggling down the back. 'What were you doing?' I said.

'Nothing.'

'No, that's not right,' I insisted. 'One of you got out of the car and took something when I was in the shop paying.'

There was a long silence and I could just imagine them, thinking that they'd got away with something that would have been in their wildest fantasies. 'I know what you were doing,' I said sternly. 'You were looking for one of those magazines, weren't you?'

'Oh no, no,' said the eldest one.

'Hand it up here.'

Now, they hadn't even looked at the magazine, because they were so terrified of going to get it that they just snatched whatever came to hand. Eventually, the magazine made its way towards me, up to the third seat, up to the second seat, up to the front seat and then to me. I took one look at it and guffawed. It was a property magazine, and the only titillating photos were of apartment complexes and duplexes. All their work was in vain, unless they were serious about wanting to rent a condo in Orlando! I can only imagine the elaborate planning that had gone into the whole thing: 'You go.' 'No, you go.' 'Now – he's not looking …' etc. All that to end up with a building magazine.

You always hope that you won't fall ill on holiday – there is nothing worse than being sick far from home, particularly if you're in charge of 11 children, but on that same trip I got a cyst on my back which was really sore and became infected. I ignored it for as long as I could, but eventually, I had to go to a clinic, along with my 11 charges, which was like something out of *Cheaper by the Dozen*. There was nobody else to mind them so I went in for a consultation, telling them all to behave while I was in with the doctor.

The doctor examined my cyst and said that it would need to be drained, but 'It's absolutely nothing to worry about, we'll just take you in overnight.'

In response, I opened the door of the consulting rooms and showed him the 11 children waiting outside. 'Unless you have a very big family hospital suite we'll forget about it.'

'I see, well, I'll schedule it for tomorrow afternoon then,' he said, and the next day, back we all went for the first of three appointments to drain the cyst and change the dressings. All good in the end, but not ideal. Normally, I have a great constitution and have rarely been ill, apart from a bout of sickness in India doing the *Grand Tour*, but it did help me to lose weight, so every cloud has a silver lining!

My niece reminded me of the final story of my Orlando adventures the other week when I was dropping her to college in Limerick. We were chatting in the car about the book and she said, 'Are you going to tell the one about *Free Willy* and the charades?' It had never occurred to me, but she said, 'You have to, it's the best charade ever.'

I remember that I took them to a teppanyaki restaurant in Orlando, which was great craic. Teppanyaki is a dining experience, Japanese style, in which the food is cooked on a hotplate and accompanied by a show, as the chefs throw knives up in the air, make volcanos with the cooking oil and fry eggs on their hats – that kind of thing. We were at a table in a private little area and I suggested that we play a game of charades after the meal. They had all played before, luckily enough, so they all got the idea. My oldest nephew stood up and did his and it was very good and then somebody else did theirs and then it was my turn. I stood up and I said it was a film and two words and I did all the actions accordingly, pointing to the zip on my trousers. No-one could get it at all: people were saying 'trousers', 'zips' – eventually, the ten-year-old shouted from the back, '*Free Willy*!' Well, the table erupted and the staff came over to see if we could stay quiet. My niece still remembers it and she's 19 now!

I know, it's a risqué story, but the point is, we had such a great time on that trip and we have memories that will never fade. That's the thing about travel – it is only partly about the places you visit and the things you see. The rest is about the people you share it with.

Recently, I went on a cruise from Rome with a few old friends and I know that we should have been excited about the lovely European destinations, like Florence and Monte Carlo, but as my good friend Mary said, 'I don't really care where we go, Francis, as long as we're together and we're having a bit of fun.' Isn't that what it's all about? And the other thing that's really important is to treat others as you'd like to be treated yourself, as the final story in this chapter demonstrates.

Once, we had an American couple coming to stay at the Park, who were booked in for a Saturday evening. We hadn't understood why they were a 'no-show', as we say in the business, until a nurse from Tralee General Hospital rang us to tell us they were in intensive care. They had had a nasty car accident on their way to us. We were horrified and concerned, needless to say, and so, two days later, John Moriarty, our barman, was going into Tralee and I said, 'Would you ever call in to see them, they have no-one.' Of course, he agreed and three or four days later, I was going into Tralee myself, so I went in to see them. They were very nice people – ten days later, they were released from hospital and they came to the Park. They weren't allowed to fly for two weeks, so we mammied them and looked after them and they had room service, and I'd hope the same would happen to us abroad. So, the time came for them to leave and they wanted to settle their bill. I said, 'No charge. You didn't cost us anything except for a bit of food,' and even though they insisted, I was firm – there was to be no charge.

Some time later, I went away and when I returned, I had a look at the hotel cheque book to see what had been happening when I was gone – I trust the staff fully but I like to keep abreast of things – and what did I see only a cheque for €635 made out to FedEx. I said to Eileen at reception, 'What's that for?'

'Oh yes,' she replied, 'I wasn't happy with that myself. I'll ring down and find out what it is.'

It turned out that a parcel had arrived while I'd been away. Parcels come in to reception but also to the kitchen and to the bar, and no-one could find my parcel. I couldn't understand what was going on, but three or four days later, I lifted my coat off the safe in the office and there was a box the size of a box of Cornflakes. Intrigued, I opened it, pushing aside the packing beads, and pulled out a beautiful black lacquered box. Inside was a magnificent Montblanc pen from this lovely American couple.

It was exceptional, but I thought, that couldn't have cost €635 euro to deliver, so I rang FedEx. The man said, 'Oh, yes, that cost €230 to deliver and there was €400 duty that needed to be paid.'

'Are you joking?' I said. 'It's a gift from guests of the hotel – I'm not paying €635 for it.' I couldn't believe the cheek of Revenue, so I phoned to enquire about the duty. I reminded the nice man who answered the phone that I was trying to help some tourists and was a bit put out to find that when you're nice, you get a bill for €635!

'Leave it with me,' he said. Three or four weeks later, he called again. 'I'm sorry, but I rang the pen shop in Dublin to get a price for the pen, and they don't actually stock it, but they told me that if they were selling it here, it would be €1,400.' For a pen! He continued, 'I'm sorry to say, the duty on that pen is €400. It's correct and we can't do anything.'

I was gobsmacked, as they say. I was going to put it in the hall of the hotel in a glass case! I still have the pen, but am afraid of my life to use it. I'm not sure what the moral of the story is here: perhaps, 'No good deed should go unpunished'!

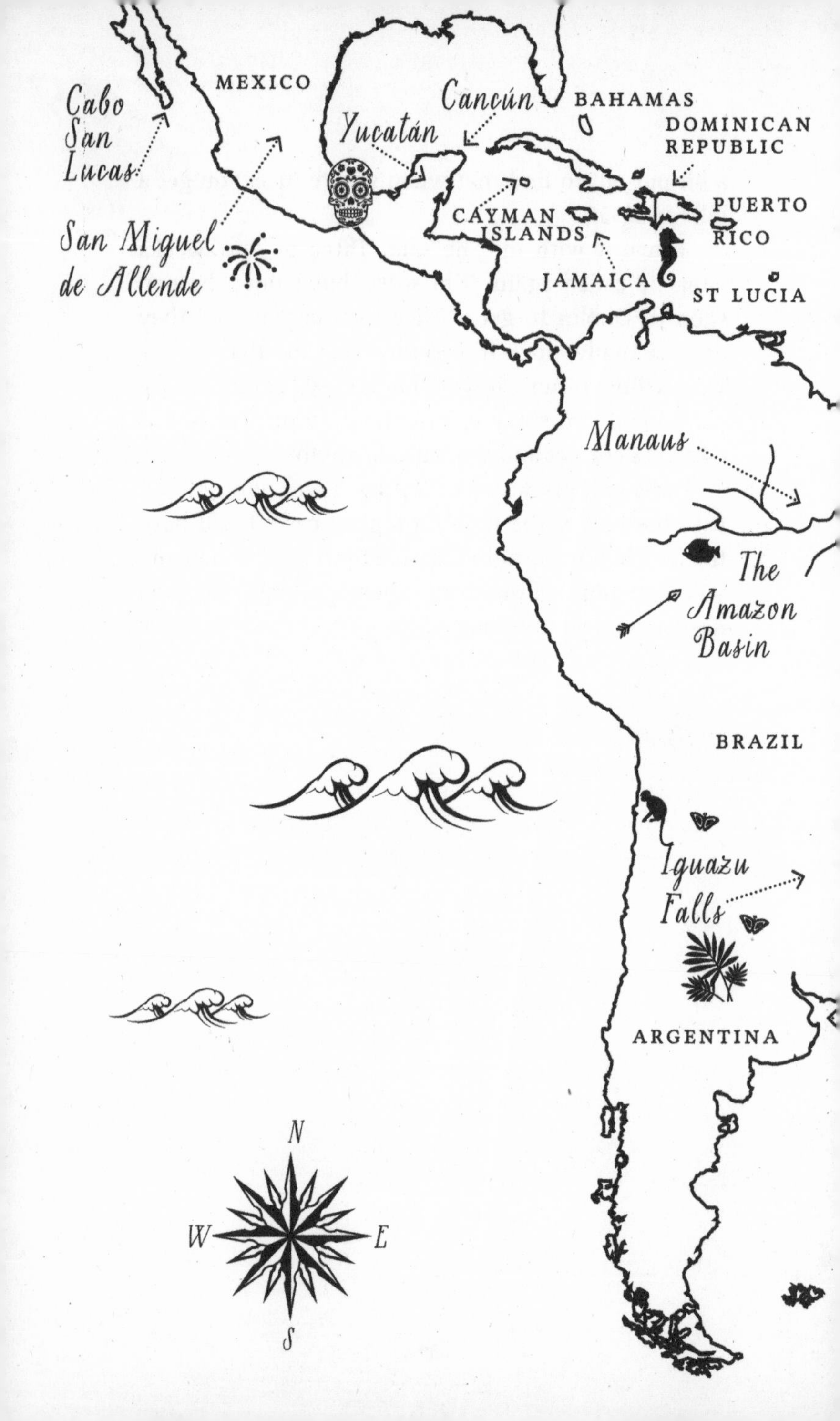
MEXICO
Cabo San Lucas
San Miguel de Allende
Yucatán
Cancún
BAHAMAS
DOMINICAN REPUBLIC
PUERTO RICO
CAYMAN ISLANDS
JAMAICA
ST LUCIA
Manaus
The Amazon Basin
BRAZIL
Iguazu Falls
ARGENTINA
N
W
E
S

From Cabo to the Caymans: South America and the Carribean

Rio de Janeiro

São Paulo

Buenos Aires

'Roots are not in landscape
or a country, or a people,
they are inside you.'

Isabel Allende

There's something so appealing about the South American attitude to life, an understanding of taking time to celebrate things, from saints' days to Mexico's famous Day of the Dead on 2 November, when people remember their deceased ancestors by constructing elaborate altars and by making offerings to the deceased. There's a special bread called *pan de muerto*, a sweet yeast bread which is offered to the dead along with things like cigarettes and even football shirts! The marigold is associated with Dia de los Muertos, as are the famous sugar skulls, and the skeleton figures that seem to be everywhere, along with faces painted to look like skeletons. So popular is the Day of the Dead festival that it's begun to catch on in other parts of the world, but for Mexicans, it involves a genuine remembrance and appreciation of those who have gone before.

We might not have a Day of the Dead here in Ireland, but whenever I go to South America, I feel a real sense of connection to the place, because their attitude to life reminds me so much of ours. Even though I love the States, I'm always aware that work is at the centre of American life, but in the continent to the south, it's all about living life to the fullest. South Americans also have a very strong sense of the spiritual in the broadest sense of the term. It's not about being religious – although many of them are – it's about a connection to something outside of yourself, something that's more powerful than you. It's also about enjoying yourself! That really appeals to me about this continent, no matter how hectic it can get.

Just like in Ireland, Semana Santa is a very important time for many South American countries, with all the rituals that surround Holy Week. Other festivals in South America date from pre-Catholic times, such as Peru's Inti Raymi, held in June to commemorate the winter solstice, and I'm told that Colombia's Baranquilla carnival rivals Rio de Janeiro's for spectacle. One experience I remember with great fondness was in Tulum on the Yucatán peninsula, about an hour or so south of Cancún. The Yucatán peninsula is in eastern Mexico, and curls around the Gulf of Mexico, and Cancún is the most popular tourist resort there – party central these days, so I'm told.

Anyway, in Tulum, a group of men clambered up a 30-metre-high pole, then most of them proceeded to swing off it with a rope attached to one of their ankles, while the remaining fellow played the flute on top. It looked terrifying and fascinating at the same time. These men, known as *voladores*, spin around like that until they reach the ground. Apparently now Tulum is a hangout for yoga fanatics and vegans, but when I went, I can assure you it wasn't! It was all about the gorgeous beaches and the ancient Mayan ruins perched on the clifftops.

Mexico has a huge Mayan heritage and when I read up on the Mayans, I realised that they are a bit of a mystery. They had this extraordinary civilisation with its own language and writing – a form of hieroglyphics, like in Egypt – and then they just vanished. My reading tells me that this may have been due to war or the fact that they'd used up the natural resources. They left behind them whole cities in the middle of the jungle, and they invented all kinds of things, including the first ball game, which involved passing around a large heavy ball, inside of which was a human skull, and the losers of the game died! They were also brilliant astronomers, and the temple I visited for the first time in the 1990s, Chichén Itzá, was built to align with the sun and stars. In fact, on one of the temples, the shadows cast by the setting sun on the steps to the top resembled a wriggling snake at certain times of the year – imagine the planning you'd need to create that. I was also fascinated to see that there was a court here for playing their deadly soccer game and, on the walls of the court, sculpted friezes showed the winning team carrying the severed heads of the losers ... The Mayans were clearly not afraid of a good fight, or a sacrifice.

Chichén Itzá was built close to two huge wells or *cenotes*, and legend has it that people were thrown in here along with offerings as a sacrifice to the god of rain – in fact, when archaeologists started digging, they found a lot of skeletons, so it must have been true!

When we first visited, I can remember that we were allowed to walk up the steps to get a closer look, but when I returned in 2014 with my Skål friends on a personal trip, the whole site was cordoned off because of fears of damage by tourists. It reminded me of what they've done with the Skelligs, which I expect will go the same way thanks to their *Star Wars* fame. They are too precious to have all of us ploughing over them.

The Yucatán peninsula is also where I had my first introduction to drones. We were staying in quite a remote place on the peninsula, near Acumal (or Akumal as it is also known), a very popular diving spot. There were eight or nine of us sitting on the beach enjoying the sun and I was reading a book when I heard a kind of loud buzzing sound. I wondered what it was, because we were very isolated and I couldn't imagine that someone was using a strimmer next door. The buzzing sound got louder and so I looked up and what did I see but a drone 100 feet above us. It went up and down the beach, then over the other side of the house before appearing over our heads again. It then took off around the circular bay, and off it went and disappeared. When we asked later, the locals told us that the police had the drone and were looking for people with drugs. Not us then!

Until I visited South America, I don't think I fully appreciated what a rich heritage it has – how full of history it is. On another occasion, I was working in California and we received an application from a hotel on the Yucatán peninsula that wanted to join the SLHW. Joining the organisation involves an inspection by an existing SLHW member, and as I had a couple of days free, I decided that I'd travel down to have a look. I flew into Mérida, the regional capital. As in many Mexican cities, the past is ever present in its colonial architecture, particularly on the long, wide, tree-lined Paseo de Montejo, modelled on a European boulevard like the Champs-Élysées. Interestingly, this boulevard was created during Mérida's boom years at the end of the 19th century, when the Yucatán peninsula produced a crop known as *henequen* – a kind of fibre that comes from the agave plant, dried out and woven. It was in huge demand at the time. Only on further research did I find that this fibre is, in fact, sisal, and the reason I find this interesting is because I was to visit a place called Sisal House, the centre of what had once been a plantation of sisal – indeed, it is located in an area also known as Sisal! Apparently, this plantation was abandoned when the sisal and jute industries were overtaken by the invention of plastic. I wonder if we'll be going back to these natural fibres now that we are beginning to count the cost of our addiction to all things plastic?

Anyway, when I arrived in Mérida, a young man was waiting at the airport, holding up a sign with 'Mr Brennan' written on it in black pen. He didn't speak a word of English, so we shook hands and he indicated that I was to follow him. We took off into the countryside, leaving the lights of Mérida behind us, until we were in pitch darkness. I was beginning to feel that it was a bit eerie, wondering if I was out of my mind, getting a lift to the middle of nowhere with a man who didn't say a word for the whole trip. We must have driven for about 30 miles until, eventually, we turned off onto a dirt road, with overhanging trees that brushed spookily off the car bonnet. Uh-oh, I thought, but after a few minutes, the gloom cleared and I found myself in front of a beautiful colonial house. It was stone built, shaped in a square around a lovely garden courtyard filled with flowers, with verandahs all around. Each room opened out onto the verandah and had lovely high ceilings and comfy sofas.

A local couple had decided to buy it and renovate and extend it as luxury accommodation. In the middle of the grounds, when they went looking, they discovered 30 cottages (all hidden under thick vegetation) that must once have belonged to the plantation's workers. Each cottage consisted of a living room with a separate bedroom, and in between the two rooms was a kind of tiny dip pool. The idea was that you'd walk down a few steps from the living room, through the dip pool, then up the steps to bed. It was an early and ingenious form of air conditioning.

When I was there, they were restoring all of the cottages and they had also discovered a wall, again covered in undergrowth, which ran all the way around the estate. When they pulled all the vegetation back, they found that the wall was about 18 inches wide with a channel cut through the middle for water to run through. Every month the plantation owners would have released water into the channel and left it there – for a reason! All the mosquitoes were so delighted to find the water that they'd come down and lay their eggs. The next day, the plug would be pulled and the eggs would drain out – a natural form of mosquito killing. I was really struck by the sheer ingenuity of this and the other ideas from a time long before mosquito repellent and other inventions. It was also the most beautiful place: I can remember floating in the swimming pool one day, watching a humming-bird hum in and out of all the hibiscus flowers for half an hour – it was absolutely gorgeous and, indeed, the whole of this unspoiled spot was heaven, with its white-sand beaches, rich green vegetation and the kind of blue sea you see on postcards.

Fireworks and Festivities

San Miguel de Allende is very different to coastal Tulum. It's smack bang in the middle of Mexico and I remember my trip there simply because the city was so spectacular and because the festival which took place there was so completely 'out there'! San Miguel de Allende is best known for its gothic Spanish architecture, particularly Parroquia de San Miguel Arcángel, which is the massive pink-and-orange church that dominates the city, and the brightly painted streets, with courtyards hidden behind grilles, revealing wonderful 19th-century houses. It's on many 'best of' lists and it's also a UNESCO World Heritage Site. San Miguel seems to specialise in bursts of fireworks in the early hours of the morning, which I witnessed once, and there are so many that they actually have a name – Alborada.

When I was there it was May and the town was celebrating a big festival, which involved fireworks at 4 a.m., elaborate dancing, a parade of horses and a giant effigy of Christ himself, complete with crown of thorns, which was paraded through the town and then set fire to. I can still remember it to this day, as they lit a fire under poor Jesus and sent his head spinning in a shower of sparks! How nobody died is anyone's guess. I was highly entertained by the black eyes and bandages the next day: the receptionist at my hotel told me that if you get hit by a firework, it's a sign that you'll have good luck that year. If your visit doesn't coincide with this festival, don't worry – there are more where that came from! One I'd love to see is the Fiesta de los Locos – the Festival of the Lunatics – in June. There are crazy costumes, a parade, sweet-throwing and, of course, more fireworks.

I know that there's been a lot of talk recently about danger in Mexico, with places like Acapulco and Puerto Vallarta now considered to be unsafe, although apparently huge efforts are being made to redress this – what a pity, as Mexico is really a fantastic place, with so much to see, and so much great food and culture. I'm afraid the only time that I encountered danger in Mexico, it was entirely self-inflicted. We were in Cabo San Lucas and myself and a pal called John Roche thought it'd be marvellous to go on jet skis. Now, if you've been on a jet ski when the sun is setting and you have your goggles on, speeding along, you'll know that when the sun catches in your goggles, you can't see anything. John and I were flying along and next thing – bang. I was launched off my jet ski into the sky and landed as if I'd come out of a cannon in a circus. John had been blinded by the sun and had hit me broadside. I landed in the sea and I have no idea how neither of us sustained any injuries. I've met him a few times since and we both agree we're lucky to be alive.

Tango Central

Argentina is very different to Mexico, but fascinating for a whole host of reasons. Like Mexico, it has a complex history, and not always a stable one. Nevertheless, I found Buenos Aires to be such a lively city. Puerto Madero is the docks area, which was in great decay when I was there, but which has now been revamped and is home to floating museums, restaurants, marinas and the glitzy financial district. La Recoleta is the Hampstead of Buenos Aires – full of tree-lined streets and magnificent buildings. We stayed in the Alvear Palace Hotel and we might have been in Paris, it feels so European. El Ateneo Grand Splendid was once a famous location to see the tango, then a cinema, but now its amazing interior, with ornate boxes and rich velvet curtains, has been transformed into one of the grandest bookshops in the world. I can't vouch for the quality of the books, because they are generally in Spanish, but the venue is absolutely worth a visit.

If you are interested in older Buenos Aires, San Telmo has lots of *conventillos*, or former tenements, I suppose we'd call them, once owned by the nobility, who then left during an epidemic of yellow fever, leaving poorer families to crowd into them. They are now trendy art galleries and shops. You'll also be most likely to see tango performed in this area, often in the open air, on the cobblestoned streets. La Boca is another neighbourhood keen on its tango, but you might also know it as the home to Boca Juniors, the soccer team, and it also has an open-air museum called the Caminito, the Montmartre of Buenos Aires, full of brightly coloured houses and street musicians. As to food, the locals love cows – eating them, that is. Beef is king in Argentina, and there is no shortage of barbecue, or *parrillada* grill restaurants. Irish people will feel right at home in Argentina. Chimichurri sauce is a favourite with steak here, a mix of herbs like parsley and oregano, lemon juice and lots of garlic, and it's delicious. Empanadas are everywhere; they're similar to little Cornish pasties filled with a savoury filling like beef or a sweet one like the dulce de leche (reduced condensed milk) that they love in Argentina.

I was lucky enough to stay in the splendour of the Alvear Palace, as I said, because I was doing a trade show for SLHW and wanted to see what kind of business opportunities there might be in Argentina. (At that time, during the 1980s, there weren't many foreign visitors to Argentina, and what visitors there were were Mexican or American. Even nowadays, air fares to Buenos Aires can be expensive and the exchange rate variable, making a holiday there potentially either good value or pretty dear.) After our stay, we were going to the airport and sharing taxis. It was absolutely teeming rain – people complain about the rain here, but in South America, rain means *rain*, and now there were sheets of it pouring from the heavens. We needed two taxis for five of us and our bags, so I volunteered to take one taxi with the baggage as it would be quicker. In I sat beside the driver and took off, going at 80 miles an hour in the lashing rain, with me in the front seat and a ton of baggage behind me. The car was aquaplaning all over the motorway, flying along, and I was thinking, well, death will be instant anyway at this speed. But, next minute, the car began to slow down, until it suddenly stopped – in the middle lane of the motorway! 'What's wrong?' I said to the driver. 'We'll be killed.' Cars and lorries where whizzing past us at top speed and every time one did, I'd close my eyes and pray for a swift departure.

The driver motioned that we were out of petrol. Sweet Lord, I thought, wondering how on earth he hadn't managed the whole thing a bit better, but then he made a calming motion with his hands, turned the key in the ignition and after a bit of wheezing, the car took off again at 90 miles an hour. *'¿Qué pasa?'* I said, summoning up my only two words of Spanish.

'Petrol and gas,' he said. It turned out that it was a dual-fuel car and he had to change over from petrol to gas – in the middle of a motorway. I was never so glad to get to the airport, which I did a good half an hour before the others, unsurprisingly.

Lost in Translation

Our next stop was in São Paolo, Brazil, on our way to New York. Sadly, we weren't going into the city, which I would have liked, because I believe it's something else. It's the third most populated city in the world, with 20 million people living in 'Sampa', as they call it. Can you imagine? But according to *Lonely Planet*, once you get past that, and the smog, you'll find a city with a great arts scene and excellent restaurants, due to the fact that it has a really diverse population, with a huge amount of Japanese people, Italians, Syrians and Lebanese, as well as people from all over South America. I'll have to go back some day.

When we got off the plane at São Paolo, we had three or four women from Mexico with us, Spanish speakers, of course, and we were now in a Portuguese-speaking country. I could see the girls ahead of us in the queue for immigration, then talking to the officials, with the chat getting louder until one of the women said, 'No, no!' In the ensuing row, I went up to see what was happening.

'They are disrespecting us,' one of the women said, 'they are using words that are not respectful.' I couldn't work out what it was that they'd said, but she was so upset she was in tears. Oh, no, I thought, wondering what I could say or do, but next thing I know, these fellows arrive in trenchcoats and the immigration officer says, 'Take them away' – or words to that effect, in Portuguese!

We were frogmarched off through the terminal building and put into different rooms, but as we were pulled along, I noticed that the rest of the group had made it to the departure lounge to wait to board the plane, so I waved frantically to signal them to take our baggage. I was left in a little room for half an hour by myself – it seemed like five, to be honest – then one of the Trenchcoats came in and interrogated me, asking me where I was going and if I was with the Mexican ladies, etc. I said, 'I'm terribly sorry, officer, I don't know what's going on. One minute, I'm waiting in the queue and I ask what's wrong with the girls, the next I'm in here.'

Trenchcoat cleared this throat and said, 'They were disrespectful to a person in uniform, which is liable to a prison sentence under section 579 ...' I was thinking, I'm in South America and I don't want to go to prison. In my defence, it was the 1980s, the height of the military regimes in the continent.

I explained that we had a connecting flight on Continental to New York, and it would be gone in a matter of moments. 'I'm worried I'll miss it.' With a shrug implying that it wasn't his problem, the man closed the door and went off.

Eventually, two other fellows in trenchcoats arrived, this time with guns. I was thinking, Oh, good Lord, this is it. I could imagine the news headlines at home: 'Kerry hotelier detained in South America', that kind of thing, as if I was a criminal who'd been hunted down! The fellows with the guns escorted me to the corridor, where the Mexican ladies were waiting. 'What on earth did you say to them?' I said in English, nodding at the Trenchcoats.

'They were disrespectful to us,' she insisted, and I suspected that I'd never really get to the bottom of this bit of lost-in-translation. The gun-toting Trenchcoats brought us down a long corridor, out onto the tarmac and onto a minibus, which zoomed under the planes until we arrived back in the terminal again. I have never felt such relief as when they let us go and melted into the background, even if we were now at the departure gate with no boarding passes. It took a fair amount of negotiation to get on the flight, which I did with a sigh of relief. I didn't like my brush with the law one little bit, even if I suspect they'd only removed us from immigration to save the original guy's face, because he had gone too far.

This little story reminds me of a later, happier trip to Brazil, in 1997, for our Skål congress. The event itself was in Rio de Janeiro, which was as spectacular as you might imagine. It has one of the most beautiful natural backdrops of any city, bar Cape Town, but I found our trip after the congress the most rewarding, because we were going up the Amazon to a native village. I was really looking forward to this trip, because I find their traditional way of life so interesting. There are a number of tribes known to live in the rainforest between Brazil, Peru and Bolivia and they are generally left alone. As recently as 2016, a Brazilian photographer, Ricardo Stuckert, took an aerial photograph of a tribe never before seen by outsiders, whose language is unknown – how amazing, when you consider how small our world is nowadays.

A highlight of my own trip was being taken in a canoe up a tributary of the Amazon for about ten miles or so, to a village near Manaus, which is the capital of the Amazon region. Manaus itself is something to behold, rising as it does out of the jungle – a city of three million people. It was once the centre of the rubber trade in the 19th century, which is why it boasts the Teatro Amazonas, an enormous pink-and-white opera house with a green-and-golden dome, filled with marble from Carrara and chandeliers made of Murano glass. It's the location for *Fitzcarraldo*, a movie immortalising an Irishman called Brian Sweeney Fitzgerald, a rubber magnate of the time (no-one is entirely sure if he existed), which has become famous for the difficulties in making it – with a rebellion by the local indigenous tribes and actors falling ill. Manaus is on the Rio Negro, and a few miles outside the city, its dark waters meet the coffee-coloured Amazon at the Meeting of Waters (not Avoca!). However, the two currents don't mingle, but instead run side by side for several miles.

The village we visited was Swiss-owned, but the indigenous people here showed us around. It's not an easy life, as the combination of the rainforest humidity and their genetic make-up means that they only live to be 35–40 years old. On our second morning there, we went on a 'medicinal walk'. I can still remember that it was about 105 degrees Fahrenheit and I thought I'd be baked alive – the humidity was overwhelming. As we walked into the jungle, our hosts explained about their use of digitalis for medication and curare, a poison placed on the tips of their arrows, for killing birds; they showed us another plant that held water, like a pitcher plant. They hunted and grew vegetables such as manioc or cassava and plantain. They are entirely self-sufficient. I was slightly taken aback recently to read a newspaper article saying that the diet of native South American tribes would make you live longer – true, it's very healthy, but the climate and hardship are no joke.

We also went fishing with them in their canoes cut out of trees, paddling along until we caught piranha fish, which we cooked on an open fire. They also had a brew that they made out of leaves to accompany the fish – I wasn't sure about it, as I'd heard about the fondness of some tribes for hallucinogens, but we remained sober! And there was no swimming with the piranhas. At night, all we did was go to bed, as there was no electricity or running water – so off we went at 8 p.m. and rose at 5 a.m., just as our ancestors would have done, and as these people still do, while we're all glued to the smartphones.

Later on that same trip, we flew to the Iguazú Falls, on the border between Brazil and Argentina. They are absolutely enormous, making Niagara Falls look small by comparison, at 2.7 kilometres wide and with 275 individual waterfalls in the system. Apparently, when Eleanor Roosevelt first saw them, she exclaimed, 'Poor Niagara!' And even though the Victoria Falls are a bit higher, the Iguazú Falls are wider. The most spectacular bit of the falls is the Devil's Throat, at more than 80 metres high.

What I liked most about the falls, however, was their setting, in the middle of tropical jungle, called La Selva in Argentina and teeming with wildlife, a welcome contrast to Niagara's casinos. There are about 500 species of butterfly alone in Iguazú National Park, as well as howler monkeys, jaguars, tapirs, giant anteaters and any number of creepy-crawlies. The jungle really does produce large insects! If you want to get away from the hordes, the Sendero Macuco is a nature trail that takes you deep into the forest, and if you're quiet, you'll see nature all around you – the flowers are beautiful. As a keen gardener, I loved to see the orchids growing everywhere. I spend an awful lot of time trying to grow orchids, so to see them just everywhere was a treat. If you're an adrenaline junkie, you can also take a motorboat – guided, of course! – out under the main falls, which looked exhilarating when I was there. Rumour also has it that there is a swimming spot near one of the smaller falls in the Selva.

On our trip, yours truly had organised a bus to the falls along with 18 others from our Skål congress. In our party were two people from Cork, who were with us on their first trip. When we got to the falls, it seemed that the whole of Japan and China was already there: it's obviously a popular stop on their itinerary, and when we got off the bus, every one of us was given a yellow rain poncho – the same as the other millions of people already there. I could really pick the members of my party out: 'Find me in the yellow poncho!' Off we went in our ponchos, descending the narrow walkways out over the cliffs, great clouds of spray rising up around us. It is really something to behold, even with the crowds milling about. We all loved the experience, but when we got back up to the top, our group of 18 had become 16: we'd lost our two friends from Cork. I couldn't find them in the sea of yellow ponchos! However, as they were adults, I had no choice but to shepherd the remaining flock onto the bus and take off for our lunch destination. Eventually, when we'd been in our hotel dining room for a couple of hours, our friends arrived in, looking slightly the worse for wear. They had got a taxi from hotel to hotel looking for us and they ate me alive – they never came on another holiday. I find that when you take a group away, and you're in charge, normally resourceful grown-ups turn into sheep – people who could run a business empire at home wander around with a glazed look in their eyes and they don't use their initiative because I'm doing it all for them!

Living Dangerously

I didn't swim at the Iguazú Falls, but it might surprise you to know that I have had some adventures on my foreign travels, not least learning to scuba dive. I know, you'd never think it, but I have. I'm not all that sure that I really enjoy it, but I feel it's something I have to do. I'd say I have a little fear of water, but it's made me all the more determined to overcome it, to 'feel the fear and do it anyway', in the words of Susan Jeffers – that's my life motto.

The first time I did scuba diving was in the Cayman Islands. They are actually more than just a tax haven! They're in the Caribbean, between Cuba and Central America, and when Christopher Columbus came across them, he named them 'Las Tortugas' or the turtles, because of the huge numbers of them on the islands – the seafarers would eat them, which makes sense. The later name of the Caymans comes from 'Caimanas', which is the Cayman name for crocodile, so they must have had plenty of those too. They are three tiny islands, and the people are lovely. They descend from fishermen, pirates and escaped convicts, but you'd never know it.

Grand Cayman is basically a seven-mile beach and if you step backward or forward, you're bound to hit water. I'd booked a holiday there with my great friend Jean and her husband, Frank. However, just before we were to leave, Jean found out she was pregnant, so she wasn't travelling and neither was Frank, so off I went on my own for ten days. I wasn't daunted by the prospect, but I did wonder what I might do to amuse myself.

I was walking along the beach one day, and I saw a sign for a dive school. They were starting a course on the Monday morning for five days, and I thought, that'd suit me grand. I've always wanted to try diving. No, I am not joking ...

On Monday morning I arrived at the beach to find that two more had signed up for the course, both men. One was a market gardener from England, the other a Swedish lad just out of the army. They were both huge, two big brutes of fellows! He'll be like Charles Atlas, I thought of the Swedish lad, and I'll be like Enid Blyton running along behind him.

The diving instructor was a lovely young girl who invited us to sit down and fill out the paperwork. I was dreading it because I thought it might be an exam, but it was only our address and insurance details, ensuring that if we drowned they weren't going to pay for us and that kind of thing. I was delighted with myself until she said, 'Now, we'll have a test. Go down to the beach. See the pier over there?' I could hardly see it, it was so far away. 'I want you to swim over and back three times and if you do it, you can start the course.

If you can't do it, I'm afraid you won't be able to do the course.'

The pier was about 500 yards away, I'd say, and over and back three times was about three kilometres! 'I can't do that,' I blurted. 'I'll be out of my depth.' (It's a rule I have: I never swim out of my depth.)

She looked at me sternly. 'You do know this is a diving course and you'll be going down 30 feet.' Well, when you put it like that, I thought.

I was discussing the merits of doing this course while the Charles Atlases were already at the pier. So, off I went doing the dog paddle and a little bit of breaststroke, because that's all I can do, and I thought I was going to faint with fatigue. I hadn't swum as much in my life ever. Eventually, I turned onto my back and kicked along a bit, until I got there. I'd made it the whole 500 metres, and now there were only 2,500 to go ... Over and back, over and back I went, and I did it. It took forever: the Charles Atlases would have made a cup of tea and had a sandwich while I was doing it!

The first night I went home exhausted. I had moved things in my body that I had never known existed. I went to bed with two Anadin at 7.30 p.m. and a pain in my chest as if there was an elephant sitting on it. I'd clearly moved my lungs like never before. I am the world's most terrified diver, it has to be said: I eat the air. Everybody else gets 20 minutes in an oxygen tank, but I get seven because I'm breathing so quickly. I do enjoy it though, honestly. And after five days I passed, with a mark of 97 per cent, so I couldn't be that bad.

On the subject of diving, years later, I went on holiday to Vatulele in the South Pacific. I know, I'm digressing, but there is a diving theme here. I was staying at a 'no-shoes' resort, and as you can imagine, it didn't suit me at all, with my foot. However, the resort was lovely: a cluster of *bures* (thatched cottages) along a magnificent beach with thick green jungle behind and glorious crystal-clear water. At the dinner table on my first night there, someone said, 'Oh, we're doing a diving course tomorrow, you should try it.' I thought, oh no. Not again. And it was an advanced open-water diving course!

The dive master, a nice Australian girl, said, 'Mr Brennan, you can do it. It's much better value, because it only costs $300 and a single dive costs $80.' Now, remember, I'm a man who likes to be able to touch the bottom when I swim, so you can imagine – here I was doing an advanced course, which includes a night dive, where the only thing you can see really is the light of your torch.

There was another test for the open-water course and this time, they brought us down to a depth of 30 feet, where they had a little obstacle course laid out for us, a set of Wavin pipes that we had to clip together to make a square and a triangle underneath the water to show that we were competent. It wasn't that bad, really, except that the waves on the surface made the water move and I banged my knee off some coral. When I came back up, my knee was bleeding. I wasn't a bit worried about it, but they kept putting iodine on it. Then, on the third day of diving, I got quite a nasty skinning of my heel when my flipper got caught, which I thought wasn't bad and put a plaster on. I use these American plasters called 'Comfort Strips', which don't hurt when you remove them – I'm like a two-year-old taking off a plaster – and they stayed on. So, all good, I thought.

On the third night of my stay, the general manager of the hotel approached me, knowing that I was a hotelier. 'Listen, I'm off for the night, can you host the table?' I was thrilled that he could get a night off and readily agreed that I'd entertain the guests and we all had a great night. But ... I was going home that night in my bare feet, holding my hurricane lamp because there's no electricity on the island – forgot to mention that! – and I had to go through a little forest to get to my cottage. And this forest was full of wild crabs. Lo and behold, one of them was clearly out on a midnight flit, because the next thing, an agonising pain shot through my foot – he'd bitten my big toe. I jumped up and began to shake my foot vigorously, whereupon he went flying off and cracked against a tree in the forest. What a pain, I thought, hobbling home – but later, I would be grateful for that crab.

When I got home, I decided to have a look at my toe and I was giving out about the crab and thinking, I'm sore somewhere, so I pulled off the plaster and there was a coin-shaped hole in my heel that was black in colour. Oh dear, that doesn't look good, I thought. I spent the night tossing and turning, and the following morning, I went into the hotel and said, 'I'm in a bit of trouble'. They had no doctor, but they did have a nurse on the island, and she got very excited when she saw it and told me that it was the start of gangrene. Oh, no, I thought, not gangrene on my leg that my mother and father worked so hard to keep. I couldn't go there.

I felt like telling them, 'You can take my other leg, but that one ...'

In the end, they flew the doctor in and he gave me two injections of antibiotics that day. When he returned the next day, he told me that he wasn't convinced that it was recovering. They wouldn't let me fly and I had to stay on two extra days, which might have been great fun normally, but not when you have gangrene in your foot. Eventually, I was wheelchaired through the airport to get my flight to New York. I had to stay with Frank and Jean for a week, leg in the air, to keep the infection away. I was on antibiotics for two months afterwards. It taught me a lesson, though. Eventually, I recovered, but there is no way I could have told Mum that I'd damaged it. Now, I wear socks inside my flippers to protect my foot when I dive. Believe it or not, I got my advanced open-water diving cert and I've dived all over the world since: Majorca, Thailand, Hawaii. I'm the world's most terrified diver, but if I let my fears dictate, sure I'd never do anything.

One final diving story, before I move onto safer topics! The SLHW conference was held on Lanai in Hawaii one year, on a resort owned by Mr Dole, the pineapple man. It's another island paradise, as you'd imagine, but it was a lot less busy and a great deal more unspoiled than the main island. It's also a great place for diving, because of the cave systems, known as the First and Second Cathedral due probably to the sheer size of them – they seemed to go on for miles. The dive master on Lanai was very good and offered to take us on a dive there.

Diving through a cave is a big deal, because it requires a lot of safety checks to make sure everyone who goes in comes back out again! With this, off we went, cave-diving. I was following the dive master when I felt something and when I looked down, there was a conger eel, about 30 feet long, swimming between us. The dive master hadn't noticed, but I sure did! I've read up on them since and am told that they are harmless, but they don't look it. However, diving on Lanai was truly special – we saw basking sharks sleeping in the caves (they'd gone in for a little rest), shoals of gorgeous yellow-and-black fish and bright orange octopi swimming along. It was unforgettable and, in spite of my fears, it was a great thrill to have experienced it.

In the Caymans, there isn't an awful lot to do apart from scuba dive and swim and lounge about – and play golf, which is perfect if getting away from it all is your thing. Mind you, I have staff that used to work for me in the Park who are now in the Caymans: I sent a few down to the Caymans for a few months when we used to close the hotel for the winter and they were thrilled, as you can imagine, to swap the rain and gloom of a Kerry winter for the sea and sunshine of a paradise island. One of them, John Hogan, went down and decided to stay. Sadly, John has passed away now, but I remember meeting him during my holiday with great fondness.

On this particular occasion, there was a new golf course and club, and John brought me along to have a look. Of course, he knew everybody on the island at this stage, and was chatting away to girl in the pro shop when two gentlemen came in and one of them said, 'Do I hear an Irish accent? I'm just back from Ireland.'

'You're right,' I said. 'Where did you stay?'

'We stayed in a lovely hotel down in the south-west, in Kenmare,' says he. 'The Park Hotel Kenmare – do you know it?'

'Oh yes,' I said, 'What a coincidence. I'm the owner.'

'I don't believe it,' he said, going on to explain that he was a friend of a famous glass-blower called Dale Chihuly and the artist had brought him down to stay in Kerry. We both agreed that it was a small world and off he went.

John whispered, 'He's a very wealthy man. He owns a big penthouse up the beach.' I didn't think anything further of it, but the next day I was in town, walking along the street, and from my right eye I saw a black car creeping along behind me. What's going on, I wondered – it seemed to be shadowing me. I couldn't imagine who would want to spy on me, but eventually, the car pulled up beside me and a voice said, 'Get in.'

I hesitated, wondering if I'd strayed onto the set of a gangster movie, but it was the wealthy man from the pro shop. 'I want to talk to you. Let's go back to my apartment.'

Fine, I thought, getting in and shifting slightly on the seat of the limousine, wondering what all of this was about. We arrived at the luxury penthouse, and when I went in there wasn't a stick of furniture, but there must have been 200 paintings stacked against the wall. On closer inspection, they were by Joan

Miró. Things were beginning to take a surreal turn and I wondered if I was now on the set of a Bond movie, whisked off the street to an apartment with nothing but priceless paintings in it.

He explained that his wife was an agent for the painter worldwide, which made me feel very slightly better, then he sat me down and got to the point. He wanted an Irish passport and in order to get one, he had to invest a million pounds (as it was then) in a business in Ireland. He had to leave it there for ten years and then he'd get his passport.

I said, 'I don't need a million pounds for anything.' He looked at me, mystified. Who doesn't need a million pounds? But what I meant was that I didn't require investment in my business, at least, investment that came from unknown sources in the Cayman Islands. Imagine explaining that to my accountant!

'Tell you what, I'll come and see you in Ireland,' he said. 'And we can discuss it.'

I thought, that's fine, I'll never see him again, but a week later, after the holidays, down he came to the Park. In order to get his passport, he had to buy a substantial residence before parting with his million quid, so I sent him off to look at houses in the area, thinking, I'm really not sure I want this. They say that there is no such thing as a free lunch, so after much discussion with my accountant, I said no. 'You're always welcome to the Park on your holidays, though,' I said.

Eventually, my friend put the money into another Irish business, let's just say. He bought an apartment down in Grand Canal Dock and made a lot of money on it. So, job done! He was perfectly legitimate, in case you ask: all he wanted was a valuable Irish passport and the scheme was open to businessmen like him, but it was on another level altogether for me.

I've always had a great fondness for the Caribbean islands and think I must have visited them all at some stage. Because of their strategic position, they have been claimed by lots of countries – Spain, the Netherlands, the UK, the USA – and so they have a really varied history and culture. St Lucia is my favourite, because it's more dramatic than the other islands, with the Pitons, two enormous volcanic mountains that stick up into the sky, and the lush tropical forest, as well as the excellent scuba diving. I have never seen so much sea life as I did on St Lucia: everything from seahorses to trumpet fish to the most colourful octopi and squid, as well as beautiful coral. Another interesting fact about St Lucia is that it has produced two Nobel Prize winners, which I found very impressive for a small place.

I have also visited St John, which is one of the US Virgin Islands, claimed by the Spanish under Christopher Columbus, then used as a transport hub for the slave trade, before being purchased by America for $25 million in 1917 – nowadays, it's a lovely quiet place full of nature and it's very unspoiled.

The Bahamas are another favourite of mine. They lie between Miami and Cuba and there are actually 700 islands in this group. When I visited, it was 1981. I was at a Bord Fáilte workshop in Miami that finished on a Thursday and I was free until the following Monday, so I suggested to Gerry, a friend from the travel business, that we take a weekend in the Bahamas – sure, why not? In those days, you could ring an airline like Delta and get a package for the weekend with hotel and air fare included, so, off we went to Nassau, the capital, to a hotel called the Rose Garden. All good, until we got into the taxi and told the driver where we were staying. 'No hotel,' he said.

I thought he was being awkward, but when he reluctantly drove us to our destination and we pulled up outside, we realised that he was right. The Rose Garden was no longer a hotel – it looked as if it hadn't been one since the 1950s. And we were in the middle of nowhere, at night. I asked the taxi driver to try a few more hotels, and he drove us around for half the night, but they were all full. Eventually, I said, 'Look, what's the biggest hotel on the island?'

'The Holiday Inn,' he replied.

'Take us there, please.'

Off we went, but when we got into reception, the woman said that there was no room at the inn, quite literally. I needed to think on my feet if we were to have anywhere to stay that night, other than the beach. I handed her my business card. 'I'm a hotelier from Ireland and I know in this hotel you have a room that's not suitable for letting, but that'll do me for the night. There's a room up there somewhere with no taps, no plugs, a hole in the roof, there was a fire in it, whatever. You have one of those rooms.' I know that every hotel has one of these rooms, because we have one of those rooms at the Park.

'I'd better get the duty manager,' she said, and when the duty manager turned up, I said, 'I know you have a room in the hotel that'll do us fine for tonight.'

'Well, we do have a room,' she said doubtfully, 'but it has no electrics.' This is often the case on island hotels, because if you run out of plugs, it might be a while before you can get hold of another one, but I reassured them that I wouldn't go near anything. So they showed us upstairs to a room full of wires and no plugs, and an extension cord was unrolled to plug a lamp into a socket outside. And we were good to go!

The girl at reception said, 'You're very intuitive.'

I said, 'Well, I'm a hotelier.' I've seen it all before and luckily, I know all the tricks when it comes to travel. We had a lovely few days in the Bahamas, waterskiing and snorkelling, and were refreshed and ready for battle on the Monday.

A group of us also stayed at the Half Moon Club in Jamaica, which is a lovely resort on Montego Bay, one of those idyllic places with a crescent-shaped beach with palm trees – just like you'd see on a holiday brochure. However, because Jamaica has endured quite a lot of gang violence, the Club is a gated community and they weren't inclined to let us out. Understandable from a security point of view, but I was dying to escape. When someone says to me that I can't do something, of course, I insist I can, and I really wanted to see some more of the island. I particularly wanted to sample some of the food, because I'd heard so much about it; it's spicy but fragrant and there's lots of fresh fish, as you'd imagine. There's also the famous jerk marinade, a lip-numbing combination of allspice, ginger, onion, thyme, soy sauce and Scotch bonnet chillies which is used to coat chicken, pork or goat, all cooked over a hot grill.

One night we decided to escape to a restaurant that I'd read about to sample some authentic Jamaican cooking, so we arranged a minibus to take us into town. The hotel insisted on sending two members of staff along with us, along with the driver, which I thought was a bit strange. As we squeezed in, I was thinking, what are those two fellows doing? When we got to the restaurant, the driver parked the minibus outside the door and we prepared to get off, whereupon the two got off and stood either side of the door, like bodyguards. Then they told us, 'Don't look right or left, just go straight into the restaurant.' What in the name of God is going on, I wondered. Of course, being me, I had to look right and left, and I saw a few fellows standing on the corner. They looked harmless enough, but when I asked a staff member at the restaurant, he told me, 'Oh, you can't stand on the street, because those fellows might make a run at you and grab your bag before you know what hit you.' Sadly, Jamaica has a reputation for violence, and even though it is mostly gang related, tourists are warned to be vigilant. It's a pity, because there is so much to see on the island, particularly if music is your thing. The Bob Marley Museum in Kingston will tell you everything you need to know about this reggae superstar.

I also skirted danger in the Dominican Republic, which is one half of Hispaniola, the island that it shares with Haiti. It's Spanish speaking and I was staying in Bávaro Beach, a lovely spot close to Punta Cana, on the east coast. I was on my own, which doesn't bother me at all: I spend a lot of time with people, at the hotel and in my other work, so when I get the chance to be by myself for a bit, I relish it. And I'm not a worrier by nature, so I never give much thought to danger on holidays – what will be will be.

I had rented a car when I'd arrived in the capital, Santo Domingo, and had driven to my resort, where I spent the rest of the week relaxing, reading and walking by the pool or the sea. When Sunday came, I asked the lady at reception where I might get Mass, and she told me that one was held in the ballroom of a hotel about three miles up the road. 'Will you need a taxi?' she asked.

'Oh, no, I have my own car.'

'You have your own car?' she said incredulously, as if I'd said I had my own spaceship! I confirmed this with the lady, got directions and off I went to Mass, which was very nice, a mix of tourists and locals. Now, the purpose of my visit wasn't just a holiday; I'd been looking at a development on the island that interested me, about 200 miles north of the resort, and I decided I'd drive up to have a look.

After Mass, I got chatting to the priest and I mentioned that I wanted to go to this place, Puerto Plata, up in the north of the country. 'Oh, are you with a group?' he said.

'No, I'm on my own.'

'How are you going to get there?' Not you too, I thought.

'I'm doing to drive,' I said, telling him that I had my own car and had planned the route through the centre of the island to the resort.

'What?' He looked at me as if I was half mad. 'You can't do that.'

'Why not?'

From his reply, I gathered that going direct from Limerick to Kerry, so to speak, wasn't safe, and I'd be better going the long way, around the Ring of Kerry! 'They'll come out of the ditch with guns and take everything you have. It's completely lawless up there.' I had wondered if the hotel receptionist was exaggerating a bit but being told by a priest was in a different category altogether. I later learned that road deaths in the Dominican Republic are very high, so maybe hiring my own car wasn't such a good idea. But do you know what? I find that it pays to be sensible on holiday and not to flash money around or look too obviously like a tourist, and not to tell the world and his wife where you're staying, but I try not to get too excited about danger lurking around every corner. If you just focused on danger, you'd miss what is special about a place. So I went on my reconnaissance mission to Puerto Plata, having taken the precaution of putting the Park Hotel on my speed dial, so if I was ambushed, I could just call and yell, 'I'm gone,' into the phone!

The island of Puerto Rico lies just to the east of the Dominican Republic and is a favourite of mine, and I was so sad to hear about the devastation following Hurricane Maria, in particular the large number of schools closing because refurbishing them is just too expensive. The island relies so much on tourism, and it's a charming place, full of old-world Spanish influences – it was another Caribbean island claimed by Christopher Columbus during one of his great voyages. He took this one from the indigenous Taíno people, who had lived there for thousands of years, hunting and fishing. Slaves from Africa formed the next influx of migrants, and, interestingly, Irish families made up some of a later wave of immigration, when the Spanish tried to squash the growing independence movement in the 19th century by inviting Europeans to emigrate there. By 1899, the Americans had invaded, keen on the large sugar crops that came from the island. Like so many Caribbean islands, Puerto Rico has a mixed history, but the many immigrants make it what it is – and the fact that there is so much history means that the buildings, like the Castillo San Cristóbal, the biggest fort in the Caribbean, are absolutely worth visiting.

During my visit there in 1986 for a Skål conference, however, we were staying in a hotel in downtown San Juan, of doubtful construction. San Juan is full of lovely colonial streets with brightly coloured houses, shady courtyards and exotic trees like banana and fig. I loved seeing trees laden with the kind of fruit you'd only see in the supermarkets here, just waiting to be picked. The President's Ball is the highlight of any Skål congress and requires full evening dress: the women bring ballgowns with them encrusted with diamanté and all manner of 'bling'. On this occasion, my friend Mary had brought three with her, hanging them on the shower curtain in the bathroom to get the creases out of them while she went off to the conference.

When she came back later that night, the bathroom door wouldn't open. It seemed to have been jammed from the inside but, with much pushing and pulling, she eventually managed to get it open a tiny bit. And what she saw was a huge pile of rubble in front of her! It turned out that there had been a leak in an upstairs bathroom for quite some time and the ballgowns had been the final straw, pulling the curtain rail and the bathroom ceiling down in the process. By some miracle, the dresses weren't damaged, but they were covered in huge hunks of mortar. The hotel, which for fairness' sake shall remain nameless, was reluctant to admit that it was their fault, as if Mary had been swinging out of the shower rail. This is a funny story, of course, and no-one was hurt, but I can assure you, I'm not complaining about Puerto Rico building regulations. During the hurricane, many buildings were destroyed, because while they could withstand category-3 storms, they weren't able for a category 4 like Maria, and also, many people simply didn't have the money to hire a builder to construct their home – they had to make do with what they had and what they had was often very little. We tend not to think about that when we are tourists in Caribbean countries.

When I read this section back, I wondered if there weren't a few too many 'danger' stories in it, and that you might all feel that this part of the world is a bit too hectic. It is full of energy all right, but that's what's great about it, that and the great mix of cultures, from the Mayans to the Spanish to the many immigrants from all over the world. From the festivals to the food, it's all about spice and fun and trying new things, whether it's scuba diving or venturing out to see things for yourself (being sensible about it, of course). As Helen Keller said, 'Life is either a daring adventure, or nothing.' Travelling in South America takes you outside your comfort zone, but the rewards are well and truly worth it.

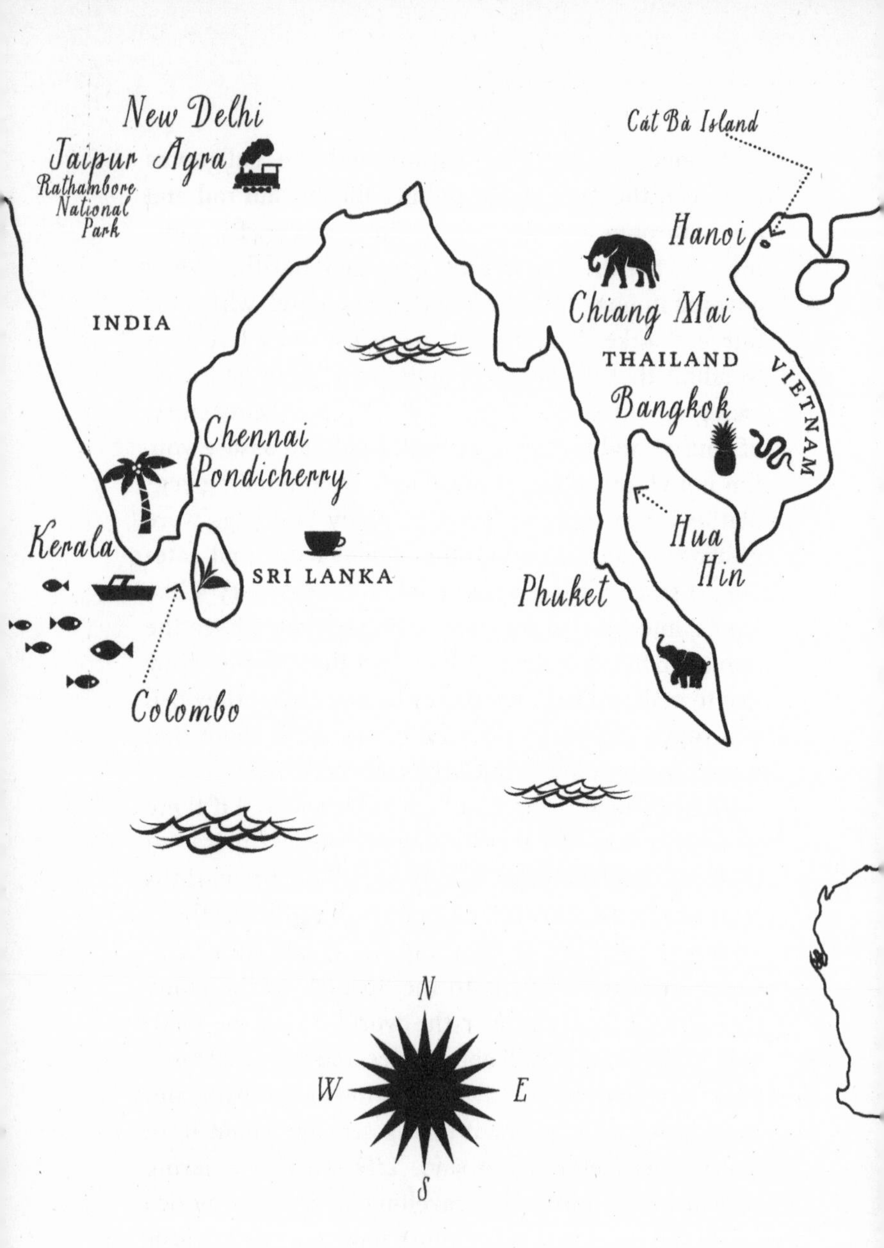
New Delhi
Jaipur
Agra
Rathambore National Park
Cát Bà Island
Hanoi
INDIA
Chiang Mai
THAILAND
VIETNAM
Bangkok
Chennai
Pondicherry
Kerala
SRI LANKA
Hua Hin
Phuket
Colombo
N
W
E
S

Tea in Sri Lanka and Other Stories: Australasia

'Those of us lucky enough to fall in love with Asia know that it's an affair that's as long as it is resonant.'

Hanya Yanagihara

I have to admit that there are many places in this part of the world that I've never visited. I've only skimmed the surface of Australia and I've never seen China or Japan. I'd love to, but the opportunity hasn't arisen – still, it's good to keep one or two countries back for the 'bucket list'! However, I know that when I'm talking about Asia, I'm covering such a range of countries and cultures, from India to Taipei, each of which is unique and very different, so I can see what the author of the above quote means – I could travel through Asia forever and still find plenty to discover.

I first went to Sri Lanka, the first country in this chapter and one of the most beautiful I've visited, for a Skål conference. (Thank God for Skål because it's brought me to all kinds of places that I might not otherwise have seen.) Even though it was very far away, it really felt like home – for a reason! To explain, after the conference, I stayed on for a holiday, and on a tour of the tea plantations in the misty centre of the island, I came across a sign for Kenmare. I couldn't believe it, in the hills of Sri Lanka! Of course, Ceylon – the original name for Sri Lanka – tea is famous but when I asked the bus driver, he had no idea why this particular plantation was called Kenmare.

I later learned that the tea industry in Sri Lanka was founded by a Scotsman, James Taylor, in 1867, on what had been a coffee plantation, with seed that came from India, and that only a few years later, Ceylon tea was fetching a record ááprice in London. It would seem that Mr Taylor had the right idea, because not long after, there was a terrible blight and the coffee crop was destroyed. Tea became the new 'gold' in Sri Lanka and planters were encouraged to come out to the island. Many came from Scotland and England and, as the plantations were frequently called after their favourite places at home, I can only assume that there must be a connection to Co. Kerry. However, the only information I could find about 'Kenmare' is that the owner in 1880 was an A. H. Thomas, which doesn't sound very Irish.

It will forever be a mystery, I suppose, but anyway, I asked the bus driver to stop and went for a visit. I was so excited by the connection that I bought two tea chests of 200 lbs each. The staff at the plantation gave me little paper bags and when I got home

I filled the bags with tea and gave them as gifts. I actually kept in touch with the tea plantation for a long time, but as the years passed, I lost touch with them. When friends were out there recently, I asked them to look, but no-one could find any trace of it. I thought that the plantation must be gone, but then I discovered that there is a Ceylon tea called Kenmare sold by a company called Fairmont and described on their website as '[a] classic high-grown Ceylon tending light with astringency and expressive flavor that has an excellent finish.' Rather like myself!

The area that I visited is called Nuwara Eliya, but is sometimes known as Little England, probably because of the cool climate, misty skies and little colonial houses. However, I also noticed that there's now a little forest park in the area called Galway's Land – another Irish connection.

Many people think that apart from tea, Sri Lanka is all about the tropical beaches – and they are lovely, but the country was terribly affected by the 2004 tsunami. One of my friends, Mary Bennett from Galway, set up a charity and channelled money through a priest based in the country, which helped a village to get a whole fleet of new boats. My trip was quite some time before the tsunami and what struck me about Sri Lanka was just how much more there was besides the beaches and how diverse it was, from Little England to thick rainforest to elephants to Colombo, the commercial capital, which is well worth a visit (the actual capital now is Sri Jayawardenepura Kotte, in case you wondered – good for Trivial Pursuit!).

When we visited, in 1990, the civil war between the Sri Lankan army and the Tamil Tigers was still on, so we didn't venture north. In fact, the conflict reminded me of that closer to home in Northern Ireland, because it went on for 26 years and many people were killed. It ended in 2009, but there are still ethnic conflicts in the country.

Like many post-colonial cities, Colombo is a mix of influences. Because it was in the middle of the ancient trade routes, it was visited many times, including by our friend, Ibn Battuta – he seems to have got everywhere! The Portuguese were the first foreigners to actually claim the city for themselves in the 16th century, followed by the Dutch in the 17th and finally the British in the 18th. This is why the city now has such a big mix of people, from the native Sinhalese to Sri Lankan Moors, descended from the original Moorish traders, to Tamils and many of Dutch and Malaysian descent. I found Colombo incredibly hot and humid, but very accessible and not as vast and sprawling as many Indian cities. The locals all walked along the promenade called Galle Face Green, a long linear park by the sea that used to be a racetrack in colonial times and is now a picnic spot where everyone seemed to gather at the weekend. The hotel to see is definitely the Galle Face Hotel – there are more modern ones if that's your thing, but the Galle Face is the colonial splendour of the city and hosted everyone who was everyone, from Ted Heath to Mahatma Gandhi. It also had the longest-serving doorman in the world, Kottarapattu Chattu Kuttan, famous for his immaculate white uniform and striking handlebar moustache. When he died in 2014, it was thought that he had spent 72 years at the hotel in various positions. I hope I last that long at the Park!

The highlight of any trip to Sri Lanka must be a train trip. Locals get around on buses, but there is a good network of trains, again a legacy of colonial times, when the British needed a handy way to get tea down from the hills to Colombo. The country's second city is Kandy, in the middle of the hill country, and the journey there from Ella in the south of the island is spectacular, as you wind your way up through the tea plantations and paddy fields, stopping at little stations and buying snacks and fresh pineapple from all the vendors waiting for the train.

A Feast for the Senses

After Sri Lanka, India's vast distances and sprawling cities come as something of a shock. I have visited the country twice, once in 2004 for a Skål conference in Chennai, the capital of Tamil Nadu on the south-east coast, formerly known as Madras. Chennai is the home of Fort St George, completed in 1640 to house the East India Company and one of the first British settlements in the country, and is now home to the state government. I really liked the city: it was certainly very hot, but it has a lot of very serene temples painted in beautiful colours and a really terrific music scene (A. R. Rahman, probably one of India's best-known composers, is known as the 'Mozart of Madras'). My next trip was filming with the *Grand Tour* in 2017, in the famous Golden Triangle in the north of the country – in 47-degree heat!

I know that it's a cliché, but the first thing you notice in India is the number of people – it's never-ending compared to sparsely populated Ireland. What I've also noticed in the time between my two trips is the change in society, as more people have been brought into the middle classes. The first time I went to the Taj Mahal in 2004 after the Chennai conference, it was busy, but not mad busy, and most of the visitors were foreign, but two years ago, with the *Grand Tour*, the difference in numbers was staggering – and the visitors were all Indian, all families, reflecting the new professional class in the country. I also distinctly remember that the first time we were there, we missed our train out of Agra and when we got to Delhi railway station it was nine o'clock at night. From the edge of the railway track to the front door of the station was a sea of people, all on the ground, taking refuge for the night. We had to step over them to get out of the station – I'll never forget it. I found it terribly distressing, clambering out over other human beings. I was upset about it for a long time, but that didn't exist this time either – it would seem that things have changed. There are poor people still in India, but a different style of poor. An Indian native might well correct me on this, but a lot of people seem to have been lifted out of poverty since my first visit.

Interestingly, when I was chairman of SLHW, one of our committee members was a Mr Oberoi of the Oberoi hotel chain, which was founded in India. Now, we always had trouble with accounting at the SLHW because, for example, cancelled bookings would be known by the hotel, but not by SLHW, even if the organisation took the booking – so accounts were always a nightmare. Worse, staff turnover in hotels was huge – it still is – so our problems never went away. Mr Oberoi said, 'Bring all your accounts to India.' It was 30 years ago and I'm afraid to say that I didn't believe him! Of course, he was absolutely correct: subsequently, the Marriott group brought their call centres to India, lured by the prospect of employees who would stay with them, and the large pool of people in the country available to do the jobs and with the right language skills.

On my first trip, we also went to Kerala, on the southernmost tip of the country, and its lovely, sleepy canals were such a contrast to teeming Delhi. When I was there, we took a houseboat for a few days – these are no ordinary barges, however. They have the same shape, but their top half is made of woven wicker with windows in arch shapes all the way along – it reminded me a bit of a turtle in the water. Some of them are more elaborate, with wooden top halves and brightly coloured awnings over the windows. There was nothing more relaxing than drifting along down the waterways, palm trees swaying in the distance.

Kochi, also known as Cochin, is the largest city. Like Colombo, it was also on the trade routes from China to the west, so it has seen the Portuguese, Dutch and British but also the Chinese, which gives it a real mix of cultures. You'll probably have seen their extraordinary fishing nets on many a travel show: the locals call them the Chinese fishing nets, and they are at Fort Kochi. Every day this row of huge nets is lowered into the water on a kind of pulley system by four men all chanting a fishing song, then pulled out again, hopefully containing fish! Fishing is what they do in Kerala, with all that water, and seafood is a big thing, with colourful snapper, squid and prawn, but there's also a lot of cooking with coconut and mango, lovely and fresh, and lots of interesting types of really light breads – and because there are so many influences, you can find just about anything in Kerala.

I'm not an adventurous eater, but I found Keralan cooking to be lighter than other regional variations and very tasty: I particularly enjoyed Sadhya, which is a kind of buffet of little curries and chutneys and rice, all served on a banana leaf. The other thing that's a must-see in Kerala is a demonstration of their martial art, Kalaripayattu. When I saw it, it began innocently enough with two fellows doing yoga-style poses on the stage: next thing, they were flying at each other with swords and shields! It looks like a mix between karate and ballet, and it's a sight to behold.

Pondicherry is south of Chennai, and again has a rich colonial history, having first been visited by the Romans in the first century AD, but was a French colony on and off from 1674 until 1954, one of a handful in India. It was the prettiest town, I remember, with brightly coloured houses and the Basilica of the Sacred Heart of Jesus, vividly coloured red and white – outside and in!

However, in India, you can't holiday in isolation from real life. I can still clearly remember going on a little bus day trip outside the city, and suddenly the driver swerved around what appeared to be a dead animal on the road. I was sitting just behind him and he looked briefly over his shoulder and said, 'Do you know?'

'Do I know what?' I replied.

'What that is on the road?'

'Is it a cow?' I said innocently.

The answer shocked me. The driver told me that it was the body of a man from the lowest caste. He'd been knocked down and killed by a lorry, but nobody would pick him up and so he would stay there like a dog on the road until he disappeared. I've never forgotten it and even though I wouldn't dream of making judgements, I found the caste system in India a struggle to understand. I suppose it would have served a purpose thousands of years ago, to put people into different strands, from the highest, the Brahmins, to the lowest, the Shudras, who did all the menial jobs, and then the Dalits, the untouchables, but I was told that in bigger cities, there is more movement between social classes these days, and the government set quotas to introduce lower castes to job opportunities. I found out that one of the presidents of India, K. R. Narayanan, was born a Dalit and had made it to the top, in spite of a very poor childhood.

Of course, real life in India is more complicated than the kind of quick judgements we make as tourists. I remember on the *Grand Tour* we were driving along through some lovely countryside and I spotted a village and, on impulse, we stopped and went to investigate. Off we went, walking across the fields of mustard and coriander plants to a village and into the home of a local family. They were a bit surprised at being landed in on like this, but they graciously welcomed us, as I've found to be the case everywhere in India. They were a 'real' family, Granny and Grandad,

Mum and Dad, brothers and sister and children, and they lived a simple life on the land, farming their crops, with nothing to their names really other than the roof over their heads. It reminded me of the kind of life my granny had in Sligo 50 years ago. The son was in his twenties and he explained that he'd get the house, but he had to look after the older generation in exchange, which struck me as being a very good idea. In India, there is a great sense of responsibility for the older generation in the younger. There was a real family bond here, but I couldn't help wondering if that would change, when their children, who were schoolgoing, would push for a university education and leave to go to the city to find work. Big changes would be coming.

It might also sound like a bit of a cliché to say that India is a country of contrasts, but it's true. There are huge gaps between rich and poor, and between the magnificent royal palaces and humble family homes. In the *Grand Tour*, we were travelling around the Golden Triangle, between Delhi, Jaipur and Agra. On our trip to Jaipur, to see the famous Amber Fort, home to the Maharajas of Rajasthan, we visited a deserted town called Fatehpur Sikri, which rises up out of the plains, a huge red sandstone complex with a giant entryway, 54 metres high, with domed turrets at the top. The wall that surrounds this city is six kilometres long, which might give you some idea of its position as the one-time capital of the Mughul Empire, and there's an elaborate mosque as well as a building that looks not unlike a wedding cake, full of tiers and arches, that housed the ladies. It was astonishing to think that after all this effort, the emperor, Akbar, simply abandoned it to go and fight battles elsewhere! But there was a more practical reason for his leaving – the lake that supplied the city dried up. To think, an entire civilisation vanished in the space of a few years.

Of course, the Taj Mahal in Agra is every bit as beautiful as you might expect, even with all of the crowds, and to think of it being built for love ... even if, sadly, it seems to be suffering some damage from pollution levels in the area as Agra itself is very industrial. I didn't notice, but there is yellow staining to the lovely white marble, and the Archaeological Survey of India has said that it needs to have a mudpack applied to return the building to its white splendour!

I also remember in particular our visit to the memorial stone of Mahatma Gandhi in Raj Ghat, Delhi. Again, there were a lot of people, but it was very moving because everyone was so quiet, contemplating the marble stone centrepiece and the eternal flame, as were we. I found that it was the same spiritual feeling as in the Skelligs and the *USS Arizona* memorial in Hawaii.

On a lighter note, we went for afternoon tea in a lovely hotel, which will remain nameless, that had featured in the film *Best Exotic Marigold Hotel*. I was dying to see it as I'd loved the film. I stressed to the gang that they had to present themselves properly, so they bought glittery tops and nice shoes and we changed on the bus and trotted off at the other end in our finery. The setting was lovely, in the gardens of the hotel, with the fine pale-stone building and a man playing an indigenous instrument. We were motioned to sit at an outdoor table and even though the afternoon tea, consisting as it did of bowls of crisps and Digestives, left a bit to be desired, the setting was magical. Mind you, the sight of us all in our finery, tucking into crisps! I had built it up as something great, but had to be told off for overselling it.

A highlight for many of the crew on our trip was the visit to Ranthambore National Park, I think because it was such a contrast to the splendour of the Golden Triangle. The sheer scale of the buildings and palaces and the sense of history are almost overwhelming at times, so it was good to get away from it all for a little while and see if we could spot some tigers. I didn't, but the crew did – they got a really good glimpse of them in the early morning. This vast park, which was once a royal hunting ground, also has crocodiles, leopards and more than 300 species of bird.

Unlike in Kerala, the spicy food in this part of India is a challenge for the Irish palate. I think we are very conservative eaters, and I know I certainly am. On my *Grand Tour* trip, I got a terrible tummy dose – some of you may have seen me stretched out on the bed in my hotel. No-one likes to hear about these things in detail, so suffice to say that I lost 12 lbs in a matter of a couple of days! And I kept them off and lost more – every cloud has a silver lining! Many people say that it's not the different food that triggers problems, but rather things like banknotes, which have changed hands many times, or door handles, unfiltered water, etc.

Loos in India can be quite a challenge for westerners, as they are generally holes in the floor, but there are some 'western' style toilets also – just make sure you wash your hands scrupulously and avoid any fruit you can't peel yourself and veg that might have been washed in tap water. Some people swear by avoiding meat, but unless you are in a vegetarian area, I'm not sure that this makes any difference. It's food that has been standing that's the problem, I'm told, not meat per se. But quite honestly, I know that I've missed out because I haven't ventured to eat that much in India: the range and variety of food is something to behold and those that did eat heartily really enjoyed it.

Travel in India is another source of fascination to me. The traffic is unlike anything you'll ever experience, with people, motorbikes, pushbikes, cars, trucks, cows, goats and everything else all piled onto the road with a ton of honking and beeping. The trains are also an experience: crowded, hot and busy, but full of life and interesting people. If you get to Mumbai, 'VT', as it used to be called (that is, the Victoria Terminus) is well worth a visit. It's now called Chhatrapati Shivaji Maharaj Terminus (another Trivial Pursuit answer), and is a great Gothic place, full of towers and turrets and home to the very first passenger train in India.

There is so much to love about India – yes, it's hot, crowded, noisy, dusty and can be overwhelming, but it's also colourful with a history that puts ours to shame, so many incredible things to see and people who are warm and friendly. Oh, and sunsets in India are beautiful. There's something about India that you just can't forget – it is such a powerful experience for all of the senses that it really stays with you forever.

The Heart of South-east Asia

Moving further to the east, Thailand is a place I've visited many times and every time I go, I love it more. There's something special in Thailand for me – the climate, of course, and the beaches, but it's also the time I've spent with friends. While other countries might be work, Thailand is all about friendship and shared time. And there's also something very serene about it, in spite of the mad driving! I can remember staying at Le Méridien in Phuket once, and every evening this man would bring a baby elephant down to the beach to play around in the water and would walk back through the hotel gardens. Apparently, he'd adopted this little fellow, and it was clear that they loved each other, with the elephant trotting along behind the man as if he was 'Dad'. That's Thailand for me.

I organised a trip there as a holiday after the Skål conference in Bangkok in 1996. Now, as you may know, the king is special in Thailand. The then-king, Bhumibol Adulyadej, was celebrating his birthday and we were delighted our visit coincided with the festivities. He has since died, having been the longest-reigning head of state in the world. After his death in 2016, the country declared a year of mourning and his cremation reputedly cost $90 million. I often wondered why the king was revered so much, but reading about him in the press after his death, it would seem that he united a country with a lot of political instability (and a lot of military coups) and many different ethnic groups. So ... when it was his birthday, we knew that it would be spectacular and that we should try to get a ringside seat to see the royal barge come down the Chao Phraya river.

By some miracle, although seats were a nightmare to get hold of, we managed to get tickets for the procession and up we sat on the bleachers by the river waiting for the grand procession. Now, we were dressed nicely for the occasion – no jeans and T-shirt. As I looked downriver, I could see threatening black clouds and in the back of my mind thought, uh-oh – hope it doesn't rain. In Thailand, rain is not for the faint-hearted!

We continued to sit as the clouds loomed, waiting for the king's barge. I could hear the chatter around us as people wondered where the king was. A police boat would pass and everyone would jump up, thinking it was the king, then sit down again, disappointed. Meanwhile, the clouds came ever closer, with the odd rumble of thunder.

Eventually, with great fanfare, we saw the king's boat coming towards us, a sight to behold, an elaborate golden barge, with what looked like a golden Buddha on the front, rowed by what must have been a hundred oarsmen dressed in flaming red. The king sat under a gold-and-red canopy. It was absolutely breathtaking. However, then it started to rain. As he got closer, the river got more and more choppy, and then this squall hit us, with the rain bucketing down and thunder and lightning. As one, the crowd began to move, jumping up off the bleachers to make their way to the street and to safety. However, it rained so much in five minutes that we got cut off on the bleachers, with a river between us and the street. We had no choice but to plough through the river, all of us in our finery. I had underpants on with a red band around the top, which immediately bled through to my white shirt – a rapper would have nothing on me! Another friend was wearing a lovely silk housecoat with buttons down the front that she'd had specially made in Bangkok, but it shrank on her and the buttons began to pop! Mortified, she was frantically holding it shut, while we sloshed back to our hotel, soaking wet. Even the king had to be rescued from the weather.

Hua Hin is about 200 kilometres south of Bangkok and after the Skål conference, I headed off there for a week, to stay in the apartment of a friend of mine, Dan Mullane. I wrote about trying to find his apartment in the *Guide to Happiness*, because it took all day and all night and involved meeting very enthusiastic locals, but Hua Hin itself is worth describing in greater detail as it really has everything. It was a popular spot for well-to-do Bangkok residents to escape the summer heat, which can be sweltering, as you can imagine, and indeed a previous king, King Rama VII, liked it so much he built himself a summer palace there in 1926, called Far From Worries Palace, appropriately enough, or Phra Ratchawang Klai Kangwon, to give it its correct title.

There was something of a building boom around the time that I was there in the 1990s, but even so, it's not overrun or too built up, and the beaches are as you'd expect, long stretches of powdery-fine sand. The countryside around Hua Hin is also lovely, lush and green, full of pineapple plantations and rice fields, with tree-covered mountains in the distance.

In Hua Hin, Wat Huay Mongkol is the temple to visit, crowned by a huge statue of Luang Por Tuad, a monk revered by many Thais, who are mostly Buddhist. I suppose you could call him the St Patrick of Thailand and this temple is full of worshippers and tourists. You can climb the – many – steps up to the statue to admire him more closely or, like the locals, you can walk underneath one of the two huge wooden elephants on either side of the statue, which will bring you good luck.

It might also surprise you to know that you can visit a vineyard in Hua Hin, Monsoon Valley Wines. I know, I didn't think wine would work in Thailand's tropical climate, but the vineyard's closeness to the sea is the key apparently, in that it's a bit cooler. Of course, I can't say I've sampled the wines, but I like the story of something unexpected working.

A final must-see in Hua Hin is the night market. It's heaving, as you can imagine, basically one long, narrow street, crammed with people and with all kinds of stalls, from their excellent street food to crafts and trinkets. The seafood in Hua Hin market is the thing, because other markets, such as Chiang Mai, are bigger on the shopping front.

This brings me to Chiang Mai night bazaar and my purchases, which ended up in the hands of the gardaí in Cork! Chiang Mai is located in the north of Thailand and known as elephant country. There's a huge night market there on the street, where you can buy, let's say, 'copies' of well-known brands by the ton and very cheaply. People seem to come out of nowhere to sell their wares and the street food is fantastic. As I have

11 nieces and nephews and they are all at that age, I bought all around me, as you can imagine – caps, pens, Nike and Puma T-shirts, the lot. After my trip, I was going to London and my friends were all were going to Dublin, so I packed my loot into a travel bag and gave it to a friend of mine, Dermot Cronin, who lives in Cork and owns a coach firm. Now, I had a lot of stuff – 'cashmere' sweaters, scarves and my knock-off T-shirts – and I had to squeeze them really tightly into the bag, but eventually I got it closed, and off Dermot went home to Cork, bag in hand. He dropped the bag into his office in town and thought nothing further about it.

Four days later, he got a phone call from the gardaí, who knew him as a local businessman. 'Dermot, are you missing anything?' It turned out that he'd had a break-in and so he went up to the office to survey the damage, then called into the station. The gardaí had two huge refuse sacks full of stuff, Nike T-shirts and scarves and fake cashmere ... When Dermot took a peek in, he was astonished.

'They must have broken into someone else's place,' Dermot said. 'I've never seen them before in my life!'

He decided to ring his daughter, Nora, thinking that the bag might belong to her, and then the penny dropped.

'Oh, my God, is that Francis's bag?' Nora said.

'It couldn't be,' Dermot said. 'There's enough here to fill two huge bin bags.' But I'm such a good packer, I'd squeezed all of that stuff into the bag.

'How on earth did you fit all of that into the bag?' Dermot asked me later. Practice makes perfect. And my nieces and nephews loved their knock-off Nike!

Chiang Mai is associated with elephants and there has been much discussion recently about the welfare of elephants in Thailand. It's a real tourist favourite, a ride on an elephant, and indeed I did it on my trip and enjoyed it, but many people are now beginning to question whether the animals are being cared for as well as they might be. I know from chatting to local people that most elephants in Thailand are captive, because they used to be used in the logging industry, but this practice was banned in 1989 and they are now looked after by their carers, known as mahouts. People in Thailand aren't wealthy as a rule and the mahouts have to feed their charges somehow, and because it costs a lot of money to feed an elephant, tourist rides pay for the elephants' keep. It makes sense in a country which relies very heavily on tourism; however, in recent years, a different approach is being taken, with experiences in elephant sanctuaries now being offered. There, people can still get up close to elephants – they can even have a wash with them! – but in a more sustainable way, with the animals' welfare at heart.

Northern Thailand is also home to some of Thailand's many hill tribes, the Karen, Hmong, Akha, Lisu ... If you are interested in cultural diversity, you'll be fascinated by these tribes and by the ways they live. However, you have to be conscious that when you are visiting these hill tribes, you are walking into someone's life to have a look around. It might be interesting for you, but it's important to be respectful – these people are not an exhibit in a museum but are going about their daily business, and while tourism might bring in revenue, their privacy is important too. Imagine if someone came charging into your living room and started poking around! Also, you might be walking into a political situation without being aware of it, so always check before you visit. I always put the camera away when I go to these places and I try to be polite and respectful at all times. If you are interested in hill tribes and want to learn more, you could try a homestay: I love to spend time with the locals when I'm visiting a country because then I really get a sense of the place. In fact, I know that on the *Grand Tour* of Vietnam, which I'll talk about next, the people who spent time in a homestay really got something special out of it that those of us who stayed in a hotel did not. They had a real sense of connection to the country and the people, rather than being on the outside looking in, as we tourists can sometimes be. Tourism these days is all about sustainability.

'Beyond the South'

This little phrase is actually the translation of the Chinese word for Vietnam, a country that used to be a great deal quieter than Thailand, but tourism has really taken hold and now it's one of the world's top destinations. I had never visited the country, so was thrilled to find that we were going there for the *Grand Tour* in 2017. In spite of its difficult history, it proved to be a lovely country, lush, green, with friendly people and fantastic food.

We began our trip in Hanoi. The French took control of the country in the 19th century, and after the Battle of Dien Bien Phu in 1954 – I remember that from my history book! – Ho Chi Minh took charge of North Vietnam. The South was an independent state until civil war broke out and the South, backed by the Americans, went into war with the North. The rest is history, as they say, even if Vietnam's progress since has been amazing. It's now one of the fastest-growing economies in Asia.

We began our trip with a visit to the Ho Chi Minh mausoleum. It's very strict and we had to line up as if we were in school or Mass, and I'm afraid we nearly got a fit of the giggles. The locals, many of whom had travelled for miles, were not impressed, as you can imagine. There was heavy security and they give you a good shove into line if you step outside it. There is no messing at the mausoleum and with its granite steps and huge tomb at the top, it felt very different to that of Mahatma Gandhi, which was a much more spiritual experience. We filed obediently along, going up one side to see his body, preserved in its glass case, then down the other. It's very like the tomb of Lenin in Moscow and indeed the mausoleum of the man the Vietnamese call 'Uncle Ho' is modelled on Lenin's tomb.

We followed this sombre trip with a visit to the Temple of Literature, a much more uplifting experience. Dedicated to Confucius, it was a centre of learning in Vietnam from the time when it was built in the 11th century. It's a huge complex of temples, gardens and walkways flanked by big marble pillars. There is also a pavilion with a statue of Confucius in it, gorgeous bright red and gold, with tiny trees at the centre. Apparently, Vietnamese students come to the temple to pray for success in exams, because it was the first university in Vietnam. They used to touch one of the ornamental turtles that line one of the pavilions for good luck, but it was damaging the stone, so they had to stop. Now, they content themselves with a prayer.

When we were there, a school tour was passing through and the children looked lovely in their immaculate uniforms, all singing a song in unison. I have to say, I was glad for the serenity because, outside the Temple walls, it was chaos! The traffic in Hanoi is absolutely mad, a swirl of scooters, cars and little vans. I have never seen so many scooters in my life! I didn't see that many traffic lights, but I was fascinated by the way the locals crossed the road, shuffling out slowly into the milling traffic, gently weaving their way through the lethal stream of vehicles until they got to the other side. There's obviously a real skill to it. If you don't want to play chicken with the traffic, there are traffic police, and they stand on a white plinth at junctions and direct the traffic. If you give them a little wave, they will get the cars to stop for you, I'm told.

Food was an absolute highlight in Vietnam. Everything is local: all the salad and veg are grown locally. Fork-to-table is fantastic there, and we could learn a few lessons here. They don't waste an ounce of land, growing herbs and salads in the tiniest corners, and with the damp climate and warm soil, everything grows! The food is light and fresh, and cooked really quickly, and a little goes a long way: a single chicken breast might be sliced very finely, mixed with a lot of fresh vegetables and rice. It's delicious and filling and with their holy trinity of lemongrass, chilli and ginger, it tastes zingy and delicious, even to my unadventurous palate! One of our most enjoyable days was spent cooking.

The water puppet theatre that we saw reminded me a bit of our *sean-nós* singing and Siamsa Tíre, in that they tell stories of Vietnam, folk stories, if you like. I learned that this tradition began in the Red River Delta of Vietnam and has been handed down from generation to generation. It involves a series of brightly coloured wooden puppets, all coated with a special waterproof varnish to keep them dry, which are placed on a 'stage' of a pond or lake surface. They are operated by little pulleys controlled by puppeteers, who are standing behind the stage up to their waists in water. Originally, the stage would have been a flooded rice paddy – and as they are everywhere in Vietnam, you can see how the tradition became popular – and performances are accompanied by traditional Vietnamese music. We didn't completely understand what was happening, of course, but it felt very special – colourful and authentic – and even though we were a bit lost, we really enjoyed it.

I know that I've spoken about how delicious Vietnamese food is and we had a fantastic morning zipping around the city going to the market, then cooking lovely fresh food for lunch, but nothing quite prepared me for the experience of going to a snake restaurant. Now, I fully understand that each country has its cuisine and indeed, snake restaurants are the highest pinnacle of haute cuisine in Vietnam, something you might save for your 50th wedding anniversary, so we were honoured, if a bit anxious about what it might taste like. Still, nothing ventured! Off we went and the way it works is that they bring you a container with a few snakes in it – they have to be farmed, by the way, for the animal lovers among you – and you pick the snake you want to eat. They cut its throat and it bleeds out – in front of you – then they dissect it in the kitchen. Some of the group were flabbergasted, but I wasn't shocked by the whole thing at all, because it reminded me of when I was a child and my granny used to kill chickens with a knife and I'd have to hold the bird down for her while she sliced the neck open. Not a bother on me.

The chef went off to the kitchen, and then returned with the snake's heart and presented it to me on a saucer. It was a little red thing, beating still, and as group leader, I was required to eat it – down the hatch. I said, 'No thanks.' Nobody would take it, and even though we felt a bit ashamed of ourselves, we just couldn't bring ourselves to give it a go, even though people in Ireland will happily eat oysters by the bucketload.

The chefs cook snake in five different ways: crispy snake skin, like pork crackling, then roasted, then in curry sauce, in a nice salad, and finally, a sushi-like presentation. As it's a delicacy, a snake dinner is very expensive, and the meat costs about $100 a kilo. I was more of a fan of the 'daily' Vietnamese cuisine, with that lovely mix of salty and sweet, sour and spicy, and the lovely fresh ingredients. Gỏi cuốn is a big favourite: rice paper rolls stuffed with coriander, chilli and shredded pork or crab. Bánh mì is one that you might have heard of because it's so 'hipster'. It's a roll, like a baguette (baguettes were introduced to Vietnam by the French), stuffed with vegetables and omelette, even pâté – and phở, that bright soup with lots of herbs, noodles and sliced pork or chicken, which can be eaten for breakfast. Street stalls will often serve cơm tấm, a kind of meal in a bowl, with barbecue beef, rice and veg, topped with a fried egg. I loved the tasty food: the flavours were irresistible.

Even though Vietnam is incredibly busy and tourism is now a big thing, I always felt that the experience we were having was very authentic, from the food to the homestay that some of the group experienced, where they lived like Vietnamese people for the night, and loved every minute of it. I think the only time I felt like a real 'tourist' was on our cruise of Ha Long Bay. This spot is the stuff of many a tourist brochure: pale blue waters studded with those curious tall limestone islands covered in green, out of which the sea has carved lovely grottoes. It's a huge draw in North Vietnam, but there are now so many cruises and so many boats in general that you wonder about the environmental effects. In fact, Ha Long Bay is in the middle of an industrial area, so pollution can be an issue. I'm not in any position to lecture, as there I was in a lovely cruise boat with gorgeous teak cabins, but it was a useful reminder that tourism often comes at a price. It would be a real shame if this beautiful spot was to be spoiled in any way.

Having said all of that, I loved my trip on a little rowing boat to the spectacular Dark and Light Cave. You go in through a long, low entrance carved out of the sea – so low, you think you think you'll lose your head as you go in – and paddle along for about 100 metres, until you come out into a spectacular sea lake, surrounded by those lush green islands. The caves are also home to little monkeys, members of a rare species that is becoming more scarce due to tourism, but if you are lucky enough to get to visit one of the islands in the bay, I'm told they are full of wildlife, from monkeys to bats and flying squirrels as well as lovely native flowers. I'm sorry I didn't get the chance to see them.

Cát Bà is probably the best-known island because of its restaurants and lovely sandy beaches and because you can travel from here to Lan Ha Bay, which is like Ha Long, but quieter. Surprise Cave is another favourite in Ha Long Bay that we did visit. It was once called 'Grotto de la Surprise' by the French, which might explain something: it is certainly a surprise when the narrow entranceway gives way to a huge cave with all kinds of interesting rock formations. One of these formations is particularly interesting and let's just say that the locals see it as a fertility symbol!

I'm not supposed to pick favourites, I know, because every *Grand Tour* has been rewarding for different reasons, but I think as far as a travel experience goes, Vietnam has surprised me the most. The food is divine and the climate, while humid, is lush and warm. I also think that the Vietnamese have been through such a lot and remain so warm and friendly. Memories of the war are distant for so many Vietnamese, probably because the population is so young. Seventy per cent of Vietnamese people are under 40, which I found unbelievable, but I got the impression from my travels that this was a country very much looking to the future and, like so many Asian countries, to becoming a real powerhouse in the region.

Adventures Down Under

I always forget that from Vietnam, it's a hop, skip and a jump to Australia, as it's that side of the world. It's a country I've visited only twice and even then only briefly. The first time I went, I spent a grand total of four days in the country as well as visiting New Zealand, which isn't enough to take it all in, but I made the most of it!

I decided to go on holiday to Australia one year after my annual month-long trip to the States, as it would tie in with some Tourism Ireland work I was doing in Australia. I planned to fly from America to Australia, but when I was in Atlanta, I bumped into Desmond Fitzgerald, the Knight of Glin, who had travelled over for an Irish Georgian Society talk – he was President at the time.

'Listen, I'm delighted you're here,' he said. 'I need someone to help me with this Irish night I'm organising.'

Now, I was only delighted to help, so I changed my flight – not realising that as I was going the 'wrong way', i.e. from east to west, I'd lose a couple of days in the process and my seven-day break would now be four. Anyway, we spoke about Georgian chairs and silver and the great and good of Atlanta were there, so, job done, as they say, even if I was feeling a bit put out at losing some of my holiday!

Thankfully, I also met Jimmy Murphy of Brendan Tours, and at the time, he was adding different countries to his portfolio, so he said, 'I'll meet you in New Zealand, if you like. I'm there to learn, so we can do all of the tourist things together.' That sounded like a good offer, particularly as he was a VIP guest of Australia and New Zealand: if he sent tours their way, this could mean substantial dollars to the tourist industry, so we were chauffeured, helicoptered and treated like royalty for the duration of our stay.

I can still remember arriving in Queenstown in the South Island, which is the backpackers' paradise in New Zealand. It's centred around Lake Wakatipu, New Zealand's longest lake, and is surrounded by snow-covered mountains, which are called The Remarkables. You might as well say it as you see it! The mountains are indeed remarkable, a bit like the Swiss Alps, and are a favourite with hikers and skiers. The lake was also used as a backdrop in some of the scenes in *The Lord of the Rings*.

It's all about the adventure in Queenstown and sure enough, Jimmy and I were doing this adventure package, where you went up a mountain on a helicopter and came down on skis, and then we got in a raft downriver, finishing with a bungee jump. The only thing I didn't do was ski, because of my foot, in case it would get injured, but I did the bungee jumping, which I'd never do again, and the whitewater rafting, which I definitely would – it's fantastic. The bungee jumping is done from Kawarau Gorge Suspension Bridge and the man who 'invented' the sport, A. J. Hackett, did his very first jump from this bridge. Famously, he got arrested for jumping from the Eiffel Tower, but I can assure you this bungee jump was legal, and safe. I'm always terrified doing things like this, but I like them at the same time, because it gives me a real sense of achievement if I face my fears.

Those of you who have done a bungee jump will know the drill: I stood there with my arms folded across my chest, as if I was in my coffin, which I couldn't help thinking I would be soon enough! They pushed me off and I fell backwards, eyes firmly closed, wind rushing past as I shot down. I was terrified that I'd hit the water underneath, but I didn't, thankfully. I just bounced up and down for a bit, feeling a mixture of adrenaline and relief that I'd done it. Now, the Kawarau Gorge Suspension Bridge is considered to be one of the smaller jumps, at a height of a mere 60 metres, but if you are really mad, you can jump from the Macau Tower – a height of more than 200 metres.

I really enjoyed whitewater rafting, though, as we bounced up and down, waves crashing down on us. It's exhilarating and fun and not nearly as terrifying as the bungee jump.

After our adventure in Queenstown, the two James Bonds went to the North Island and to our next destination, which was a place called Huka Lodge on Lake Taupo. It's a luxury retreat with lots of outdoor activities, including helicopter rides, but it's probably best known for its fly fishing. It was actually founded by an Irishman called Alan Pye, who was attracted by the excellent fishing, and the river has been fished by none other than Queen Elizabeth II.

I'm not a fisherman and neither was Jimmy, but we decided to give it a go and off we went at seven o'clock in the morning, hiring a little boat on the lake. It truly was beautiful when the sun came up and the mountains were all around us. The lake is heated from geothermal springs, so the fish feed on huge amounts of plankton, which means they end up being around three or four pounds in weight, which is very big for trout. We caught a few and came back to shore to barbecue them for breakfast. That lovely flesh was a pinkish colour and the skin was crispy and charred; I have never had a nicer breakfast.

This area is really wonderful if you like nature: the Huka Falls are a phenomenon, as all that water from the Waikato River comes down a very narrow channel, thundering along, and it's a great place to hike and to mountain bike, as well as to drink wine, as there are lots of vineyards in the area. Even though I don't drink, I enjoy having a look around! I did love the geothermal pools, though, and taking a dip in one of the many natural pools in the area is a must, as is seeing the bubbling mud in the Craters of the Moon, a place where you'll see a lot of geothermal activity and big clouds of steam rising up into the air.

We continued our journey through New Zealand's geothermal heartland with a trip to Rotorua, a bit further north on the North Island. Its full name is Te Rotorua-nui-a-Kahumatamomoe, and it was founded by Māoris. It is home to lots of sulphur baths, thermal springs, bubbling mud pools and magnificent geysers, such as Pohutu, shooting hot water high into the air, and Te Puia, which is also home to the New Zealand Māori Arts and Crafts Institute, essential to understand the history of this place. You can also visit a traditional Māori village and see how Māori people used to live, as well as getting a chance to see their famous 'haka', or war song, the one the All Blacks chant at rugby matches. Their sacred place is the *marae*, or meeting ground, where they will mark important tribal occasions, and you can visit one with an organised trip. The carvings in the central meeting house, or *wharenui*, are absolutely spectacular, and they also tell stories about the tribe and its history.

Rotorua is also known as 'Roto-Vegas', because of its little strip by the lake, which is probably a bit of a grand claim, but still – they have a sign in the style of the original and iconic Las Vegas one, so they are obviously keen!

(Because of all the sulphur, there's no escaping the smell in the town of rotten eggs. Nothing wrong with that – it is nature, after all – but it reminded me fondly of two women I'd worked with years ago in Jury's hotel in Ballsbridge. It was one of my very first jobs, as night manager of the Coffee Dock, which at the time was one of the few places that stayed open late in the city. It was frantically busy, I remember, and some of the staff were real characters, including these two, who were real mammies, but with a streak of divilment. One night, they decided to investigate the contents of a box that had been put on top of the fridge and left there for five months – to discover that it contained gone-off egg whites. They only found out when they upended the box on themselves, but not before the smell filled the restaurant. It was so bad the customers thought we'd had a gas leak and I had to call the fire brigade!)

We finished our trip in Auckland, which is the biggest city in New Zealand, with a population of about one and a half million. It resembles Dublin in many ways, not least because it's surrounded by mountains and the sea, and it's very vibrant. You can't visit Auckland without taking a boat out on the bay and after our day working there (yes, we did work!), we were treated to a sailing trip, which was lovely, even if I did get burned alive. I was as red as a tomato. I'm not good in the sun: I have to work on a tan slowly, but like an eejit, I didn't know how hot the sun was, nor did I think about the reflection off the water, and I ended up with a shocking dose of sunburn; I spent the next 24 hours taking aspirin to keep my temperature down.

My favourite memory of New Zealand comes from another trip, however, one that I took after our Skål convention in Cairns in Australia in 2002. I travelled with a friend, Margaret Gainey, a lovely woman who owns Crag Cave in Castleisland, Co. Kerry. The caves are thought to be a million years old and they have a great collection of stalactites and stalagmites, extending over more than three kilometres. I often joke with Margaret that she's the only woman in the world who makes money out of a hole in the ground! Having said that, I really admire her for transforming it into a lovely spot, with a visitor centre and children's parties. So, anyway, Margaret was terribly excited about the trip, which we'd begin by flying to London, which is also where our problems began. She wanted to jump up immediately and join the queue for the gate, but as a seasoned traveller, I'd have three chapters of a book read while waiting to board, so I said, 'What's the rush?' but I let her go on, before correcting myself and following her when I realised I'd been a bit rude.

The computer had broken down and they were handwriting boarding passes, which should have made me suspicious, and sure enough, when we got on the plane I thought that it was very full for a business flight to London. I located Margaret, who was sitting in a different seat row to me, and told her to stay put, sliding my briefcase under the seat and having a good look at the chaos all around me. The flight was jammed and people were crowding on, attempting to shove bags and coats into the overhead lockers, then bagsing seats before the next people could nab them – there was no allocated seating. Eventually, in the melee, we gathered that the flight now had an overflow of 42 passengers. What had happened was that they had been issued their seats before the computer broke down, and when it did, the whole allocation had been re-issued, so there was a total of 42 double-ups. And because it was a late flight, nobody was getting off. And I mean nobody. The captain had to come on air and offered people €200, then €400, then the last group went for €600. The cattle auction took two hours and our flight was dead late. I wasn't terribly bothered because Margaret and I were only going to London for our flight the next day, but I can still remember meeting a family with children on their way to South Africa via London. At the time there weren't a lot of South African flights, so timing was crucial, and this poor family were about to waste a mid-term trying to get there.

The long and the short of it was we had to be re-booked onto our Australian flight, so we had 24 hours to spend in London, but on discussion, Margaret and I decided we weren't that keen. Then I had a brainwave – 'Let me try Singapore Airlines' – and I booked the two of us to fly to that city at 9.10 the following morning en route to Australia. We had a lovely day in Singapore and Margaret never forgets it because she got to the famous Raffles Hotel for a Singapore Sling! This famous drink was invented by a barman at Raffles, Ngiam Tong Boon, and is a mix of gin, cherry liqueur and fruit juice. Raffles is one of the great colonial hotels of the world and is associated with a whole host of famous literary types, including Somerset Maugham, who, according to a piece on Singapore in the *New York Times*, 'was said to sit beneath a fragrant frangipani tree in the hotel's Palm Court and craft short stories from tidbits of gossip overheard while supping among Singapore's gentry.' Thankfully, after trying a bit too energetically to clean up Singapore's reputation as a den of iniquity during the early 20th century, the country is beginning to enjoy its history again and Raffles is now a national monument. The country is even restoring the old and infamous Bugis Street, which was home to much carousing during the Vietnam War, and was famous for its transvestite ladies of the night. On a more genteel note, Singapore is also famous for its Gardens by the Bay, a wonder of a natural park, which is probably most famous for the Supertrees, giant tree sculptures planted with a whole range of green plants that act as oxygenators of the air. Sadly, this all happened after my visit – I'll have to go again to see it.

After our lovely day in Singapore, Margaret and I flew onto Christchurch in New Zealand, where we met up with the rest of the Skål gang. They greeted us both with lots of stories and chat and off we took from the airport over the mountains, heading towards one of the many glaciers at the other side through the Southern Alps. As you can imagine, the scenery is out of this world – and you can take a train from Christchurch, the Tranzalpine, if you want to see it all, but we were taking a bus.

Unfortunately, as we drove into the mountains, it began to make very strange noises and one of the party, Dermot Cronin – he of the overstuffed bin bags of designer goods – who runs a bus company and therefore knows about these things, said, 'This bus is going to break down.' All of a sudden, the bus stopped. 'Didn't I tell you?' said Dermot. At this stage it was getting dark in the New Zealand equivalent of Glencree, so we were all a bit nervous. Off Dermot went to confer with the driver and returned to tell us that we needed water for the engine radiator.

I said, 'I'll get looking,' because I was only delighted to have a job to do. A few of us clambered out of the bus and crossed a sheep-filled field or two to find a river at the bottom of one of them. All we needed was something to carry the water from the river to the bus, so we got our Duty Free bags and emptied them of bottles and perfumes, along with a very smart bag from my friend Mary Bennett's lovely gift shop in Galway. We decided to have a competition to find which bag would hold the most water. Sadly, Mary's deluxe bag leaked like a disaster! Still, I suppose she never thought she'd have to fill it with water in the middle of nowhere to fix a broken-down bus. Anyway, we filled the radiator with water, the driver got the bus started and off we went back down the other side of the mountain. We never had a bit of trouble after that. However, it was a real eye-opener to see the mountains and the glaciers on the South Island and to be reminded just how close it is to the Antarctic. Well, it's still 5,000 kilometres, but that's an awful lot closer than Ireland is! And Wellington has the honour of being the southernmost, and most remote, capital city in the world.

The two glaciers that people visit the most are the Franz Joseph Glacier and the Fox Glacier (called after New Zealand's 19th-century prime minister, Sir William Fox), which is a vast river of ice in the Southern Alps. It's best visited by helicopter, I'm told, which we didn't do, but you can also take a guided hike. The Franz Josef Glacier is called after the Austrian emperor, and if this puzzles you somewhat, a German explorer who discovered it named it after him. I think that the Māori name, 'Kā Roimata o Hine Hukatere', is much nicer, as it translates into 'the tears of Hine Hukatere', a Māori woman whose partner was swept away in an avalanche while they were out climbing the glacier, according to legend. Very poetic.

We finished our trip right down at the bottom of the South Island, by observing some of the country's native penguin population, which was a wonderful experience. New Zealand has a number of penguin families, including the tiny blue penguins, the yellow-eyed and the Fiordland Crested, with its lovely tufts of yellow on its head. You can see them in little spots along the coast, notably at Oamaru, sometimes known as Penguintown, and at Dunedin, where they slide onto the beach after their day's fishing expedition. Dunedin formed the setting for the film *The Piano*.

My visit to Australia was just too fleeting a trip to count, sadly, although I did get to re-enact my favourite TV show, *Nothing to Declare*, in a brief stopover in Sydney. It shows the work of Australian customs officers, and I'm always astonished at what people try to bring in to the country. Mind you, Australian customs officers mean business! We were flying from Auckland to Sydney and on the plane, we were handed our landing cards to fill out, complete with questions about whether we'd been on a farm, etc. I was compliant, because I knew better, having seen the TV show! No ostriches in my backpack ...

When we landed, we were going through the system and to my surprise, I got pulled to one side for a bag check. The officer looked at me unsmilingly: 'Do you have anything in the bag?'

'No,' I said. I was sure, because I never carry much in my suitcase – I'm a light traveller.

My friend rooted around in my suitcase and after some rummaging, he held out a bar of Cadbury's Dairy Milk that I'd forgotten about. It was one of those finger bars that you can't get any more – I was a big fan.

'What's this?' he said, holding it up.

'It's a Dairy Milk.'

His eyebrows lifted.

'It's a bar of chocolate,' I clarified, in case he hadn't heard of Cadbury's Dairy Milk.

'What else is it?'

I didn't understand the question. 'Well, it's something you eat when you want a treat.'

He glared at me, then pointed to the form. 'It's food. You can be prosecuted for this.' I was thinking that 'food' meant only legs of lamb and rashers and sausages, but I was wrong. 'It's food and we asked you to declare it, but you told a lie to an officer on your form.'

There was a long silence while I felt like a naughty schoolchild. Eventually, he sighed and said, 'I'll let you go but be more careful the next time.' I went off without my bar of chocolate. Having had experience of customs workers, I was very nice and didn't argue, all the while thinking, oh, you eejit. I knew better than to say anything, though.

I do have one abiding memory of Sydney, though, when I visited the city briefly for an AGM of the SLHW in 2010. We had a lot of meetings, and after three days of sitting inside looking at the views of Sydney Harbour, someone mentioned at a coffee break that there were tours of Sydney Harbour Bridge. We all got very excited and decided to book one, but were very disappointed when our local tour guide told us that it was booked out, because they only do small groups at a time.

'Oh, well, we're the board of the Small Luxury Hotels of the World. We're very important,' we insisted and that sort of nonsense. So, our guide got on to the mayor, no less, and word came in that they'd open an hour early to take 12 of our group. All well and good, except that there were 13 of us. We decided to pick names out of a hat, and sadly, mine didn't get selected. I was a bit disappointed, but that's the luck of the draw, I told myself. And besides, the next day's meeting wouldn't begin until 10 a.m., to accommodate the tour, so I could have a lie-in.

Now, there was a fantastic party that night in the Sydney Opera House, and we had a tour of the building, all dressed in our finery. I had been dying to see the Opera House up close, because I'd read so much about it, and it really is as impressive as the pictures suggest. It was designed by a Danish architect, Jørn Utzon, in the 1950s. UNESCO says, 'It stands by itself as one of the indisputable masterpieces of human creativity, not only in the 20th century but in the history of humankind.' Standing in front of those giant sails, you'd agree with them.

At the party, quite a lot of drink was taken, except by yours truly, of course. As usual, I was home early and off to bed, while the rest of them caroused. When I got up for breakfast the next morning, I was very surprised to see the tour bus pull up to the hotel at 8.45 a.m. and the gang get out, all dressed in white jumpsuits (you wear them on the bridge, so you don't catch any loose buttons or belts in anything). 'God, you're back quick,' I said.

They looked a bit shamefaced and then the story came out. They'd been picked up by the bus and taken to the bridge, and the safety manager had looked askance at one or two of them. Now, before you climb up, you have to blow into a breathalyser to make sure you're not drunk. Everybody in the SLHW group had had to blow in and guess what? Every single one of them was drunk. The only sober man on the board was at home in bed! Now, they were back, chastened, having wasted everybody's time and given a bad name to the board.

We left Sydney, tails between our legs, for Cairns, right up in the north of the country, and went scuba diving on the Great Barrier Reef. One of our colleagues from Galway was very keen to buy a camera, as you did before mobile phones took over, but even though we kept pointing shops out to him, he would shake his head. 'No problem,' he said, 'When I get to the Great Barrier Reef I'll buy one.' He thought that the Great Barrier Reef was a place with shops, not a natural phenomenon! Luckily at that time, 2002, the Great Barrier Reef was still in good health and relatively pristine – not like today – and I'll never forget how beautiful it was, with all of the colours and the little fish. Mind you, when I first got to Cairns, I couldn't understand why all the quaint, old-fashioned streets had canopies over them, but I quickly realised that it was because of the intense heat – in December it would be 40 degrees.

I'm sure I'll get the chance to return to Australia and see a bit more of the country, but I know that I'll certainly go back to Asia again and again, because it's so different from the rest of the world and because the huge range of cultures is very special. It really is so full of energy and the people are determined to be progressive, but at the same time, they respect their history and their traditions and they really believe in family, which reminds me so much of home.

Stockholm
SWEDEN
DENMARK
Copenhagen
UNITED KINGDOM
London
POLAND
Scilly Isles
Paris
Vienna
AUSTRIA
Zurich
FRANCE
SWITZERLAND
ITALY
Lourdes
Rome
Naples
Pompeii
Mount Vesuvius
Capri

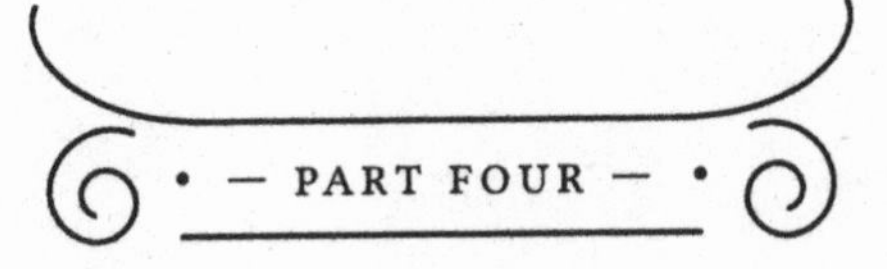

PART FOUR

Foie Gras and Cockscomb: Europe

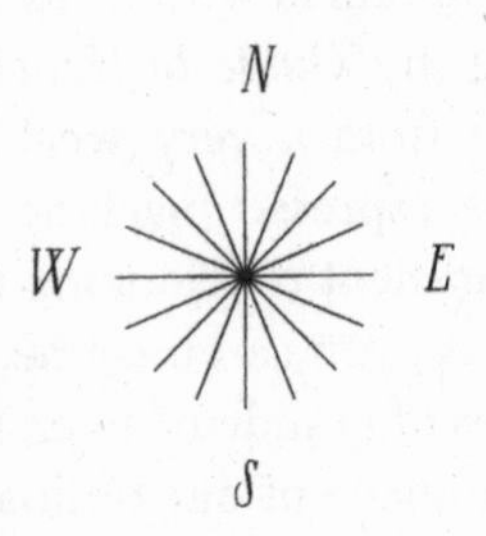

'One never goes so far
as when one doesn't know
where one is going.'

Johann Wolfgang von Goethe

America might be the country I know best, but my earliest travel experiences were in Europe. I can still remember going as a 17-year-old with my sister Kate to a Paris wedding as guests of Claire Wagram, who had spent many summers with us as a student. Those of you who read my *Guide to Happiness* may recall that Claire came from a very wealthy family, who had invented the espresso machine, and lived in a chic Parisian apartment overlooking none other than the Eiffel Tower. As you can imagine, this experience gave me delusions of grandeur! Even though I used to wonder what she made of our ordinary family home in suburban Dublin, she once told me that she loved it and used to look forward to spending time with a family like mine, who sat around the dinner table every night and ate together and chatted.

When Kate and I went to Paris, I was completely swept away by the beauty of the place and by the fabulousness of the wedding, held in the Bois de Boulogne, in a private house – it would probably be the equivalent of the American ambassador's residence in the Phoenix Park. The pre-wedding and wedding and post-wedding parties were endless and glamorous – the groom was Claire's brother and he was marrying a girl from Hawaii, who needed to be baptised, make her Holy Communion and be confirmed before marriage, with a party to mark each – so by the end of it all, Kate and I were completely exhausted. I have to say, it spoiled me for travel forever after! I could fully understand what Audrey Hepburn meant when she said, 'Paris is always a good idea.'

(We didn't see a lot of Paris on that occasion, but mention of the city reminds me of a funny story. We were doing another show years later in Paris for Bord Fáilte and a well-known Irish hotelier got a little overexcited and didn't come home till late. The next morning, we were all set up for our event, which was a kind of speed-dating affair, where travel agents move from table to table every four minutes, and you tell them about your tour or county or hotel. The table in front of mine was due to be filled by this hotelier, but of course, it was empty. Quick to improvise, I said, 'Someone sit in there and talk about what he's meant to be talking about, until he shows up.' So someone, I can't remember who, sat in and an hour or two went by and eventually he arrived, the worse for wear. Uh-oh, I thought, wondering how long he'd last. He was sitting in front of me, and I'd see him falling forward every now and then, face hitting the table! There were a few alarmed looks, but nothing further, and I worked away, talking about Kerry and the Park Hotel Kenmare, when there was a thump and a scream. He'd fallen forward on the table, out cold, and his toupee had gone flying off into the lap of one of the travel agents. She'd let a roar out of her, as you would, and he was quickly removed.)

After my unforgettable trip to the wedding, I can clearly remember stopping off to visit the famous Chartres Cathedral. Its full name is the Cathédrale Notre-Dame de Chartres, and it's dedicated to the Virgin Mary. It was magnificent, I remember, with its two Gothic spires rising up out of the flat countryside. I can only imagine what 12th-century pilgrims would have made of it. It's probably best known for its stained-glass windows and natural light is filtered through them, so you can picture how beautiful it is. At the centre of the cathedral is a maze of passageways, which, we were told, Catholic pilgrims used to follow on their knees to emphasise their devotion. Unfortunately, Kate and I disgraced ourselves by getting a fit of the giggles while we were being led through the cathedral by our guide. I can still remember Kate exploding with laughter when the guide explained that the ground sloped away from the altar because they used to wash it down in mediaeval times – I have no idea why she found this so amusing, but once we'd started, we couldn't stop. 'If the two of you can't behave yourselves, can you please leave?' the guide said. What is it about having to be on your best behaviour? It always seems to bring out the worst in me, anyway! I felt a bit guilty, to be honest, because I'm normally very well behaved in church, but in my defence, I was only a youngster. We had to go back to the bus to wait for the rest of the group to join us, like two bold children.

My next foray into the world of travel was Interrailing after doing my Leaving Cert – a slight departure from the luxury of a mansion in the Bois de Boulogne! But before I relive the discomforts of that trip, my laughing in church story reminds me of another time I was seized with a fit of the giggles in the house of God. Every year I go to Lourdes with the Kerry Diocesan pilgrimage – it's a trip I love and I wouldn't miss it. I love to attend the Masses and vigils and I'm happy to do the big pile of washing up that always follows the group meals. I'm a demon washer-upper. Before we go, we have a raffle to raise funds to take this group to Lourdes and the winning ticket gets a free trip. We all buy tickets and one year, a lovely girl who worked with me in the Park, let's call her Cindy, won, having bought a ticket from me, so I was delighted. (She married a porter at the hotel and they have a lovely family now.) Anyway, I was telling her all about the trip and I mentioned that on the fourth or fifth day, they bless any objects that you've brought along, such as medals and rosary beads. You don't have to have the object with you for it to be blessed – when the time comes, you can simply think of it and it's done. Another important factor in this story is that holy water is ordinary water that becomes holy when it's blessed, but Lourdes water is already blessed when it comes out of the ground. I don't need to know how or why, I just know this to be the case. Bear with me ...

So, we were all in the basilica having the blessing ceremony and everyone holds out whatever it is they want blessed – I had a couple of medals I'd bought for the family, so I held them up. Just before the blessing I hear the door of the church banging and walloping and we all turn to see what's going on. There's Cindy coming through the door with two 25-gallon containers filled with water, which she had collected and brought up to her hotel, up a very steep hill, then up five flights of stairs to her bedroom, then lugged it back down the stairs, out the door of the hotel and back up the hill to the church. Cindy is a Kerry woman and is tough out, but even so ... 50 gallons of water! I hadn't the heart to tell her the job had already been done. When it got back to Kerry, it was doubly blessed!

Now, back to the Interrailing, which I touched on in my *Guide to Happiness*, but which I relived for this book, thanks to the diaries I keep. I have one for every year from 1966. They're not the kind of diary where I pour out my feelings, and I'm glad about that. I'm not like Oscar Wilde, who said, 'I never travel without my diary. One should always have something sensational to read in the train.' These diaries aren't sensational, but simply little mementoes of what I did on a particular day that are great fun to re-read, even if I couldn't recall some of the many things I'd done. Memory can be a funny thing.

When I picked up my little 1974 diary, though, it was like stepping back in time. Brian Duffy (an old friend of mine from schooldays) and I decided we'd do Interrailing. If you think that sounds unlikely, you'd be right, but I was only 20 and I had been working in a place called Marlin Communications, selling TV aerials, so I thought, why not? Maybe it was time to see a bit of the world outside Ireland. I finished up in Marlin and we headed off for the month of July. We began in France because, in order to maximise the ticket, we could count Le Havre as Day One and have the full 31 days.

We wanted to go places we'd never been, so after a day or two in Paris in unbelievable heat, we headed for Denmark as our first 'proper' country. We took couchettes – very posh – on the night train from Paris to Copenhagen and arrived in Tivoli Gardens on 4 July. They are the original 'pleasure garden', opened in 1843, a wonderland of trees, parkland and fairground rides, from the original 19th-century carousel to the modern roller coaster. They also hold concerts there and have all kinds of curious buildings, from a pagoda to an Indian-style temple. They are rumoured to have been the inspiration behind Walt Disney's Disney World; Hans Christian Andersen is also thought to have spent a lot of time there. I can still remember their old-world charm, but the grotty hostel we stayed in I've thankfully erased from my mind. I wasn't a natural for Interrailing, to be honest. I'm not a snob by any means, I'm happy to say, but I like to travel comfortably and to stay in nice hotels. They don't have to be five star, just cosy and comfortable and, more importantly, to be booked well in advance. The 'by-the-seat-of-your-pants' style of turning up in various places and trying to find a hostel was not my style then and it isn't now. I like to be organised.

My little diary informs me that we also went to the Tuborg brewery, which I enjoyed. I can still remember the cheesy beer adverts of the 1970s, so that's what must have inspired me! I also joined the many people who flocked to the statue of the Little Mermaid, which is probably Copenhagen's best-known landmark. She's called Den Lille Havfrue, for you Danish enthusiasts, after the fairy tale by Hans Christian Andersen in which a mermaid is told that if she wants to become human, she will lose her voice for ever. The statue is quite unimposing, but it has been a huge tourist attraction since it was completed in 1913. It has also been a target for vandals, having been decapitated a couple of times, blown up and most recently covered in bright red paint.

On 6 July, we crossed over the sea from Denmark to Sweden. Today, we'd take the Øresund Bridge, but it wasn't built at the time so we took a ferry and then headed for Stockholm by train. We were thrilled to be going to Sweden, thinking it was terribly exotic, but our first experience was traumatic. (Many years later, I returned to Stockholm with my priest friends from CUS, and we stayed in a hotel called the Berns, which had the most beautiful room I'd ever stayed in. It was small but perfectly designed, with a lovely restaurant, where they served authentic Swedish food – no meatballs, I can assure you: it was very cutting edge.)

We pulled into a place called Södertälje – the name is imprinted on my brain – and when I looked out the window, I could see this man running madly up the platform. He didn't look in the best of health, so my first thought was, poor man, before returning to my book or newspaper. The train was very crowded, so Brian had had to find a seat in the next carriage.

Just when the train was about to leave, the man clambered on and came into my carriage and sat down beside me. He didn't say hello, so neither did I – I can remember finding the Swedes more reserved than us chatty Irish folk – and I continued to read and to stare out the window. Then I heard a funny noise from my fellow passenger and I thought, oh, he's fallen asleep. The next minute, he slumped forward in his seat, then fell to the ground. Nobody spoke a word of English and I didn't speak any Swedish, but I cried, 'Help!' and tried to pull him back onto the seat. He was a blue colour and he was pretty much gone, I know that now. I ran down the train looking for anyone who might help and came across some soldiers and I said, 'Can you help?' They had CPR skills and they worked on him but he was gone.

The train had pulled to a stop at the next station and didn't move, because the authorities needed to come on board to check on the man. As I had witnessed the death, they had to get an interpreter to question me, and I had to make a statement, and we stayed there that night. It was so expensive I couldn't believe it. The next day, we headed towards Stockholm, and everything got dearer and dearer as we got closer. We thought, we can't stay here, because we'll use our full budget in a week, but I have to say, the incident with the man had really shaken me.

So we turned around and got a ferry to Poland, then took a train through Poland and on down to Austria before continuing our journey to northern Italy and Venice. 'Not a nice city,' my diary declared at the time! I suppose it was 30 degrees and the height of the tourist season and I had my backpack on – can you imagine? The hostel was horrible and it wasn't cheap! I've been back since and stayed in the Danieli, and it's much nicer: it's a 14th-century palazzo near St Mark's Square, the famous Bridge of Sighs – or the Ponte dei Sospiri – and the wedding-cake beauty of the Doge's Palace, so, right in the centre of things. It's typically Venetian, with a lovely pink stone front and elaborately carved window surrounds, as well as a magnificent courtyard and staircase and a terrace with a view over the lagoon and all of the islands. Everyone who is anyone has stayed at the Danieli, from Ernest Hemingway to Richard Wagner to Charles Dickens, from George Sand and Maria Callas to Harrison Ford, among many others. It's magical, but when the city is hot and overcrowded and people are pouring into St Mark's Square, you are not seeing Venice at its best. If you get the chance to go to this wonderful place, try to do so earlier in the year, when it isn't as busy.

From Venice, the two of us found our way via Rome to Sorrento, having first experienced the madness of Naples. What is it they say? 'See Naples and die!' In fact, it is thought that Goethe may have first said this and that the quote should read, 'Once one has seen the Italian city of Naples, one can die peacefully, since nothing else can match its beauty.' The setting is certainly spectacular, with the curve of the bay and the volcano of Mount Vesuvius in the background, but sadly, Naples in the 1970s was beset by problems, from toxic waste dumping to the Camorra or mafia, and when we visited, street crime was at an all-time high, but it has a fantastic archaeological museum as well as being home to the original pizza – and it is a great stopping-off point for the Amalfi Coast and Pompeii.

My diary records reveal that I wasn't all that taken with Pompeii, which I described as 'boiling' – and it was. I couldn't take in anything of the tour that we went on: the guide was talking but every time I found an arch, I hid under it. However, I do recall feeling a bit cheated by the whole experience. In school, we had been led to believe that the ash fell on everybody just as they were and that they were frozen in time, but now I discovered that this isn't quite right. If ash falls on you, you're burned to a cinder and the ash hardens around what *was* you, but is now a kind of vacuum. What the authorities did then was to pump in plaster of Paris so that when the ash was removed, it looked like a fully formed human, rather than someone who had been erased from the face of the earth. So the famous bodies of the humans at work and the dog on the lead aren't 'real'. But then I learned that the site itself had been rebuilt, because of course it would have been ruined during the volcano in 79 A.D., and was bombed during World War II – so maybe it was better to see it as a kind of model of a Roman city, and it was certainly very impressive and moving to imagine people in their final moments like that.

I can still remember visiting my sister, Kate, who was on holidays in Sorrento at an actual hotel, unlike the two of us, who were slumming it, so we used to go every day and sit by the hotel's swimming pool – much more like it! Having said that, the Amalfi Coast is beautiful in a truly romantic way: lots of clifftop villages tumbling down to the sea, the best-known of which are probably Positano, with its ice-cream-coloured houses all clustered together between the mountains and the sea, and the wonderful little village of Nocelle at the top of 1,700 steps – not for the faint-hearted, but the views over the bay are out of this world. John Steinbeck wrote about Positano for *Harper's Bazaar* in 1953 and his essay is well worth reading if you get the chance: he evokes the place so well, from driving along the world-famous Amalfi drive, called the Nastro Azzurro, or Blue Ribbon, barely wide enough for two lanes of traffic, the sea hundreds of feet below. The journey had him and his wife clutching each other in fear, he recounts, and he describes the characters in this place, which was then little visited, 'a dream place that isn't quite real when you are there and becomes beckoningly real after you have gone'. Very true. What I found most surprising is that when he visited, Positano was poor and shabby with no visitors – something that would seem extraordinary now.

If you like walking, the Path of the Gods – Il Sentiero degli Dei in Italian – will take you high up the mountains, and I was amused during my research to find that hiking these trails is considered the preserve of 'Germans and Anglo-Saxons'. I'm sure they'll let Irish people in too! If you have vertigo, you might not like the sheer drop to the ocean below, but you'll be rewarded by the stunning views of the mountains, the sea and the winding road that takes drivers along the coast. It will also give you a very good idea of what the area's many invaders, from the Greeks to the Barbarians to the Romans, saw in this place. In fact, Emperor Tiberius took refuge on the isle of Capri and built himself a home from where he ruled his empire in his old age, the lucky man.

I can still remember my trip by boat out to the island, seeing it rise up out of the blue sea – it's very steep and looks a tiny bit like Gibraltar, which is perhaps why Napoleon took it as a base for the French fleet, but not before it had been occupied by everyone from the Turks to the Romans. My diary records that we paid a visit to the home of Axel Munthe and this had me scratching my head, because I have no idea who he was! I later (re-)learned that he was a Swedish doctor who visited Capri as a student and noticed that there was a crumbling villa there, San Michele, and vowed to return when he could to restore it. This he did, and he wrote a book called *The Story of San Michele*, which was a bestseller at the time and is still in print. The villa contains all kinds of treasures collected by the good doctor, from Etruscan art to Renaissance paintings, and I remember the vine-covered terrace, which was so serene. Apparently, Sweden's Queen Victoria used to visit Dr Munthe regularly and her little dog is buried at the villa.

Capri is also known for its extensive Roman ruins, including that of the emperor Tiberius's Villa Jovis, which must have been huge, judging by the outline of the walls that remains. He built no fewer than 12 villas on the island, and they were rumoured to have hosted all manner of debauchery. Capri is also famous for style, and the *Independent* described it as a 'fashion victims' paradise', which it is now, with its designer shops. Like so many places in Italy, it is completely overrun in the summer, so I'd advise a visit in the off season, so you can savour the beauty all by yourself.

Roman Holiday

My diary tells me that Rome was incredibly hot, as you'd imagine in July, and Brian and I did all of the tourist things, from the Trevi Fountain to the Vatican – of course – and the Colosseum, which is every bit as spectacular as you'd imagine. It was just out of this world to stand there and imagine 80,000 people all roaring at the top of their voices. Interestingly, when I mentioned this to a friend, her 13-year-old son got terribly excited and provided me with all manner of facts about the Romans and the Colosseum. He told me that in Roman times, the Romans would hang a crucifix above the gate to the gladiatorial arena to mock the Christians before they got eaten by the lions, and if this didn't provide entertainment for the masses, the poor Christians would be put into the chariot races and even if they won, they'd die! It's lovely to see that history still excites teenagers these days.

If you visit Rome, you'll undoubtedly find the Colosseum jam-packed with visitors, so a quieter place, but well worth seeing, is the Palatine Hill. It's one of the famous seven hills of the city and it is thought that Romulus, the founder of Rome, came from a cave on the hill along with his brother Remus – you'll probably remember the legend from school, about the twins who were cast out on the banks of the Tiber and taken in and raised by a wolf, before Romulus killed Remus in a battle over where the city was to be built. The emperor Caligula – a terrible man – was assassinated on the Palatine Hill and it was also home to the emperor Augustus and his wife, Livia: you can visit the house of the emperor and admire the colourful frescoes.

Of course, Brian and I visited the Trevi Fountain, like any tourist – but we didn't recreate *La Dolce Vita* in it! My diary also reminds me that we visited the catacombs as well – now, they have discovered even more of these underground burial sites, but when we were there, they were still very impressive. They were built by Jewish people in the first century AD and later, Christians also buried their dead there. According to rumour, the Holy Grail is buried there, but this theory is thought to be a bit far fetched!

The Vatican City is one of my favourite places in Rome because there is so much to see and do, and because the sheer scale of it is so impressive. Those of you who saw the *Grand Tour* episode set in the city will no doubt remember me running around like mad, trying to shepherd my gang around and encourage them not to get lost. This is because the Vatican is enormous but also because the production itself is quite demanding, so I have to be on my toes at all times. During filming, we have a production meeting at 6.30 a.m., which consists of the camera man, sound man, director, myself and a couple of PAs, to discuss the day and where we're going. We have a strict schedule to adhere to: if we're meant to be filming at 7.30 a.m., we can't arrive at 8.45 a.m.. Also, we're dealing with foreign languages, permits, traffic and distances between places, so, while it might look as if all we're doing is sitting on a bus on our holidays, behind the scenes is very different.

When we arrived into Rome for the *Grand Tour*, we reached our hotel at 4.20 p.m., whereupon I learned that we were going to film at the Vatican – right that minute – and that I was to be wearing 'tomorrow's clothes'. This means I had to wear the same clothes as for the next day's filming as this segment would be part of that – it's all about continuity. However, I had been in the Vatican recently on a private tour and it takes about seven hours, and this was late on a Friday afternoon. What would you be doing, I thought, but I understood that the director wanted to get ahead on things, so I changed into 'tomorrow's clothes', took half the group with me, and off we went to the Vatican.

Now, I had said that I needed a guide to the Vatican, because even though I've been there three or four times, I can't remember the details of dates and architectural styles, what's Renaissance and what's Baroque, that kind of thing. Finding things like a guide is the job of a 'fixer', a local person at the location who arranges all the necessary filming permits and takes care of the practical things.

Those of you who have been to the Vatican will be familiar with the line of white stone cobbles delineating the border between the Vatican City and Rome – it's a nice photo opportunity to pose with one foot in each – and of course, all the gang did so, even though I was trying to get them to follow me. I was walking along with the man who had been introduced to me as the guide and I said, 'Can you tell me what the two fountains are?'

'No, I don't know.' He had very limited English, so it didn't bother me, even though I thought it was a bit odd for a guide. I said, 'That's fine – what's the obelisk in St Peter's Square?'

'I don't know.'

Sacred Heart, I thought – call yourself a guide?! Then I wondered if he was one of those guides who knows the quirky things, like how many cobblestones are in the square, that kind of thing, so I said, 'How many cobblestones are in the square?'

He looked at me, astonished. 'I don't know.'

'What do you mean, you don't know?' I said. 'Aren't you the guide?'

'No, I'm the fixer,' he said.

Holy Mother of God, I thought, I am going into the Vatican on camera with a fixer. I had to think on my feet, so I said, desperately, I might add, 'Do you know a guide?' As I said this, there I was, looking around St Peter's Square, as if someone might emerge from behind a statue to rescue me!

'No, well, my mamma, she a guide,' the poor man said in his broken English.

'Does she live near here?' There are six people and a camera coming at me and I haven't a clue.

He shook his head – 'No, she's at home,' and he motioned far into the distance.

'Does she have a phone?' I said.

He shrugged. 'Of course.'

'Well, I'll tell you what,' I said. 'You phone your mamma and get her to stay on the line. I'll say, "What's that?" You ask your mother, "What's that?" And then you tell me.'

He nodded and took out his phone to ring Mamma and we were off, cameras rolling. 'What are the two fountains?' I asked him. He muttered into the phone in Italian, then said in English, 'They're by Bernini.'

'What is the obelisk?' He asked his mother, and I was told, in wonky English, that it was brought back from Egypt as a spoil of war, and that the doors to St Peter's Basilica are made out of copper, melted down from the ceiling of the Pantheon many centuries ago. Into the Vatican I went, asking my questions and getting an answer via Mamma, translated from Italian into English of a sort. It worked, but sweat was pouring down my back and the poor fixer looked as if he'd never recover. *Bella Mamma!*

Edelweiss, Edelweiss ...

The next stop for the two backpackers was Switzerland, a trip which still gives me nightmares. Not because Switzerland isn't lovely – it is – but because we ended up getting robbed. I suppose it's a rite of passage for any backpacker, but even so. I can remember that Switzerland was terribly expensive, and very picturesque. We began in Interlaken, which has been a tourist destination since the 19th century, because of its fantastic views of the Swiss Alps, including the Eiger, and the two lovely lakes that surround it, the Thun and the Brienz. Our old friend Goethe visited – he seems to have got everywhere – and Mendelssohn was also to be seen taking the mountain air. Interlaken is also famous for the railway that will take you all the way up to the top of the Jungfrau, a height of 3,454 metres, or 11,332 feet. The railway is famous for the 'windows' which have been cut into a tunnel, through which you can see the north face of the Eiger. It's wise to check the weather before you take this railway, though, because it can be very misty at the top and you might not see anything. Mount Schilthorn is another popular destination, because of the views of the 'Jungfrau massif', as they call it, which includes the Eiger. Apparently, some of *On Her Majesty's Secret Service* was filmed here and there is a James Bond themed revolving restaurant at the top.

From Interlaken, Brian and I travelled on to Lucerne, which is a chocolate-box town right in the middle of Switzerland, surrounded by mountains and, of course, Lake Lucerne. You can take a cruise on the lake, which is ringed by mountains, and there are lots of swimming spots if you're keen, and if you are feeling adventurous, you can take a cable car up one of the mountains. One of these is Mount Pilatus, which also has a terrifying little railway journey to the top, with gradients of up to 48 per cent, so not for those with a fear of heights! It's called a 'cogwheel' railway, because it runs on two adjoining wheels, like those in a clock, and that's how it manages to cling to the mountain. It was the brainchild of a man called

Eduard Locher, an engineer with ambitions, and his little train was a wonder of the world's fair in Paris in 1889.

Chur is where the nightmare began for us. It's the oldest city in Switzerland and near St Moritz and Davos, so, *très chic!* It is a complete fairy-tale town, with winding cobbled streets and pretty churches and with the mountains stretching above it; it is another one of those picture-postcard places. And the old town is car-free, so you can really enjoy it in peace. The only drawback was that Brian and I were staying in the usual hostel, one of those packed places with bunk beds in tiers, three high. Oh, well, we thought, it was clearly the price to pay for being in such a lovely place.

The next morning when we awoke, there was a bit of a kerfuffle and one girl was crying – it turned out that she had been robbed during the night. Brian had put his wallet into his pillow slip, thinking that he was being extra careful, but it, too, was gone. The robber had broken into the hostel and had cut open his pillowslip with a knife when he was asleep and stolen 30 Swiss francs from his wallet. We had to wait for the police to come: they told us that this fellow had been travelling through the country, robbing as he went. Shaken, we left Chur that day and travelled to another gorgeous little town, Schaffhausen am Rhein, which is on the border with Germany and, apart from the Pinot Noir grape, is best known for its waterfalls (which are 75 feet high and almost 500 feet wide, the biggest in Europe, I'm told), as well as the Munot Fortress, a very imposing place designed by Albrecht Dürer. I can also remember that the town itself was full of vividly painted baroque houses, some with incredible detail.

After next stopping off in Lausanne, Brian and I returned to Paris, which we left on 1 August to return home to Dublin. I swore that I would never rough it again. But even though it's not for me, I can see that it's a fantastic way to discover a lot of places in a little time and to experience a bit of life, which we most certainly did. Later that month, I was working in Redmond's off-licence in Ranelagh, near the Triangle, and I went off to get my Leaving Cert results, to discover that I hadn't got enough to get into college. My working life was to begin and the last real summer of freedom ended.

Many years later, I was to return to Switzerland, and I'm not sure my trip was any more auspicious! I was doing sales calls in Europe at the time, during the mid-'80s, and I arrived into Zurich at 4 p.m., in just enough time, I thought, to pay a quick visit to the Aer Lingus office. The station manager, a man whom I knew well, said, 'Oh, Francis, I'm delighted to see you. We're having the Galway Oyster Festival European Championship here in town and I've no Irish judges. Would you do it?'

'I don't know the first thing about oysters,' I replied – it's not strictly true. I did help to put together the Kenmare Oyster Festival, but I wasn't about to let my friend know.

'Sure, you're Irish,' he said. 'You'll be grand.' As if being Irish gives you a degree in oysters ... Anyway, my friend said cheerfully, 'I'll give you a clipboard and a pen and you'll look the part.' I was told to go to the Dolder Grand Hotel, a typically Swiss hotel with lots of towers and turrets, at 5 p.m. that afternoon and they'd organise everything for me.

When I arrived at the hotel, I was given a white coat as well as my clipboard and pen and I looked very official. I was to observe European master chefs shucking and preparing the oysters and to pretend that I knew what I was doing. In spite of my organisation of the Kenmare festival, I have to confess that I've never eaten an oyster in my life, nor will I ever ... but why let that stop me?! The winner would appear at the Galway Oyster Festival that September, so the stakes were high. My fellow judges and I ticked the boxes and one man broke an oyster, so he got no points, and another man didn't shuck correctly, so he lost out, and so on ... (there were no women in the competition, as at the time, kitchens were really dominated by men, which is happily not the case any more).

When we finished I removed my white coat and heaved a sigh of relief, looking forward to going back to my hotel for a nice cup of tea and a rest. But my friend had other ideas. 'Now, you're joining us for dinner tonight.' I can't stand barging into parties. I hate it: if I'm invited, fair enough, but if I'm not, I find it all a bit embarrassing, so I said, 'I wasn't on the guest list, so I'm not coming.'

'Will you stop it, he insisted, 'You're a judge and you have to go.' It looked as if I had no choice, and I suppose I should have been delighted, because the restaurant had a Michelin star and was very highly thought of. So, that is how I ended up with five French speakers in this exclusive restaurant, me the fake oyster judge with my E in Leaving Cert French, nodding away and '*oui*-ing' and '*non*-ing' to my fellow guests.

The menu is still imprinted on my mind: foie gras to start, followed by Vichyssoise soup, which is basically leek and potato soup, blended and generally served cold; next, rillettes de veaux, which is a kind of pâté (made with veal in this case, but it can be made with pork or duck or anything, really); langoustine, which is Dublin Bay prawn, and that layered sponge and chocolate creation called a 'religieuse' for dessert. All fine, but there was one item on the menu I didn't recognise, something called 'crête de coq'. Maybe it's chicken wings, I thought hopefully.

This restaurant was exclusive and all the food was served under cloches, which I'd never seen before. I'm convinced that there is a cloche mountain somewhere, because the idea was for the birds. If you have to serve each dish under this silly silver hood, you have to have a waiter for each plate – so five waiters were needed for my table! It did remind me a bit of *Fawlty Towers*. Also, nobody knew what was under the cloche, so when it was whipped off, we had to look at what lay underneath and marvel. I thought, in the name of God, what's going on here? I was way out of my depth.

Foie gras came and my fellow guests were oohing and ahhing over it, then the Vichyssoise, which they said was *merveilleux*, and then it came to the main course. The waiters lifted the blessed cloches and we all prepared ourselves ... It seemed to be a dish of sweetbreads, which was fine, along with a solitary Dublin Bay prawn and this white parsnip – a tiny baby one, mixed with tiny carrots. The dish was accompanied by three balls of pommes Parisienne – basically melon-scoops of crispy mashed potato – you wouldn't want to be Irish! I'm not the most adventurous eater, so here I was, thinking, I don't like any of this, while my fellow guests were saying, '*C'est magnifique*'.

I nibbled away at the sweetbreads, which weren't bad, then ate a potato and a baby carrot, all ok, then I tried the crête de coq and it tasted like an elastic band. I chewed and chewed, and it only got more rubbery, and I thought, Sacred Heart, how on earth will I swallow this?

One of my dining companions leaned over to me and asked, in French, if I was enjoying my meal.' '*Oh, oui*,' I said, '*Mais, qu'est ce que c'est?*' I managed to add in my rudimentary French, pointing to the crête de coq on my plate.

'*Oh, je ne connais pas le mot, mais ...*' and he pointed to the top of his head. The penny dropped – it was the cock's comb. It was truly the most unpleasant thing I'd ever tasted. I went home at 10.30 p.m. and ate a Mars bar!

Semmelknödel

All of this food reminds me of the time I ate soup and dumplings for eight days straight during a tour of Austria. It's a lovely country, but I can clearly remember completely losing it in the house of Viennese aristocracy after being served the dish for the umpteenth time. I wrote about this in my first book, *It's the Little Things*, how I collapsed in the kitchen with repressed laughter while an astonished chef looked on, but my trip to Vienna for a Skål congress in 1988 provided me with lots of material – I could write six books about that trip!

It didn't get off to the most auspicious start when we arrived at the airport, all excited about the trip to come, and formed a queue at check-in. One of my great friends, Nano Flannery, was there with her husband, Frank, who has since sadly passed away, and as we all stood there in the queue, I noticed that she looked upset. What's wrong, I wondered, deciding to go up to her and see.

When I asked her if everything was all right, she looked around her frantically and whispered, 'I've brought the children's passports and I've left ours at home.' She showed me two passports that were both in the name of 'Flannery', but not those Flannerys!

'Oh, For God's sake, come back here,' I said, assembling us so that we were a group of 12 and gathering all of our passports into a big pile. In those days, you had a real ticket, so I marched up to the check-in desk with 12 tickets and the girl checked all of the tickets first and gave them back to me, and then I put all 12 passports up on the counter like the Leaning Tower of Pisa. I could hear the collective intake of breath from behind me as she picked them up and looked through them all. Without a word, she nodded and handed them back to me. Thank you, God, I thought, ushering the gang on towards the departure gate.

Of course, we were only over the first hurdle, because when we landed in Vienna, we'd have to show our passports to immigration control. This was during the Cold War, when passports were scrutinised a lot more, so I said to Nano and Frank, 'Now, you two stay on the plane and you're to be the last off, because I'm going to run up to the arrivals hall to see if we can get through.' Off I went and when I got into the terminal, I looked down into the arrivals hall, which was full of phone-booth-style passport cubicles, with an official in each one – not good for us! I'd have to think quickly, so I went back to the group and told them my plan. 'Now, we're all to head towards the same booth in immigration control and when I say, "*Trína chéile*," start chatting and dropping things and making a bit of noise and pay no attention to the man in the booth.' Off we went and when we arrived at the booth, we all started going mad with the chat and noise. I had the 12 passports and I walked up to a booth and said, 'The Irish group,' loudly, handing him the whole bundle. The man looked at me as if I was dope of the month, but I pressed on. 'We have the bus waiting, don't we, Mary?' I said to no-one in particular. 'We have a bus,' I repeated, and everyone nodded and agreed.

My goal was to cause confusion and slip through the net, but what did he say only, 'No, no, one person, one passport.'

'Oh,' said I, 'I didn't realise that.' I turned to the gang. 'When I call your name, make sure you come up here now.' Now, I had a bottle of gin in my hand, which I'd bought for the others in the group. When I turned around, I made sure to drop it, accidentally on purpose, and it spilled all over the floor.

'Oh no,' the man said, and clambered out of the booth.

The *trína chéile* started and in the commotion, I whispered to Nano and Frank, 'Just go.' They sauntered through, not a bother on them, while your man was still panicking about the gin and I was busy apologising and over-explaining.

We weren't done yet, though. The 12 passports were up on the shelf of the man's booth and somehow I had to extract the Flannery passports out of the bundle. The others were still milling around the passport officer, who was trying to clean up the mess, so I saw my chance, grabbed the bundle, lifted the two Flannery passports out of it, then said, 'All right, when I call your name, come and get your passport,' and they all came forward, took a passport and wandered off. The passport man was only delighted that I was helping him out, even though we were now minus the two Flannerys, who were home safe. It was a triumph, even though I say so myself, and luckily a colleague who joined us for the conference later brought out their passports, saving us from the same pantomime on the way home.

The plan was that after the congress, we'd do a tour of the country, visiting a different city every night. We began in Vienna and in a fit of enthusiasm, I booked a night at the famous Vienna Opera, to see a production of *Mary Stuart,* a tragic opera by Donizetti. *Maria Stuarda* in Italian, don't you know! I was mystified to find an Italian writing about Scottish history, but my research tells me that the composer was fascinated by the Tudors, and composed *Anna Bolena* and then *Lucia di Lammermoor,* which is based on a Walter Scott novel. It was spectacular, even if we were only slightly up to speed with what was going on! Of course, it ends with Mary Stuart being led to the chopping block – and my head nearly joined hers, because I led the gang out at the wrong metro station and we had to walk all the way to the opera house through the snow, in full evening dress. We all agreed that it was worth it, though, for the spectacle.

Vienna really is the most beautiful city, with its enormous palaces – a legacy of the Habsburgs – including the Schönbrunn summer palace, with its wonderful gardens stretching off towards the horizon, filled with elaborate fountains, and magnificent gold-painted gallery. You approach the palace across a vast cobblestoned square and its scale is hugely impressive – it really does give you a sense of the power of the mighty Austro-Hungarian empire and of royal families at that time. Another interesting fact about the Schönbrunn palace is that it was the meeting place for John F. Kennedy and Nikita Khrushchev during the height of the Cold War.

Many Europeans are familiar with the Austrian Empire because of a famous trio of films based on the life of Empress Elisabeth, or 'Sissi', who was married to Franz Joseph – unhappily, which clearly provided material for all of those films. They starred Romy Schneider, an Austrian-born actress, who was later to make a great career in France, and the films are a Christmas institution in German-speaking countries, a bit like *The Wizard of Oz* is here.

If high culture is your thing, you will love Vienna. Their national gallery is stuffed to bursting with Old Masters and, of course, the city produced composers from Beethoven to Brahms. It is also home to cake, which might be on top of other people's to-do lists! In fact, we stayed at the Sacher Hotel, run by the Sacher family, who also created the famous Sachertorte, a chocolate cake coated in rich icing, of which a tiny slice is perfect with a cup of coffee.

Later in our trip, we ended up in Salzburg, home of the famous yearly opera festival. We were staying with a fellow Skål hotelier who had open access to the venues and arranged for us to get a tour of the main opera house, the Festspielhaus, and to look at the stage that so many, including Maria Callas, have sung on. It's one of the best venues in the world, so we were terribly excited. At the time, the opera house was being refurbished and all the seats were being replaced and the theatre was a hum of activity and clattering and banging. Our guide showed us the technical area and before we knew it, we'd wandered on stage. Looking out into the vast theatre, I remember thinking, oh my God, imagine ending up on that stage, singing in front of all of these people. Impulsively, I turned to the gang and said, 'We have to sing,' and we burst into a rendition of 'Molly Malone'. It wasn't exactly Montserrat Caballé, but all the workmen gave us a round of applause!

On the same trip, we were taken over the border to Interlaken in Switzerland to go to a casino owned by one of the Skål members. They gave us a big disc as a gift and we were allowed to put it into the fruit machines for a free go. We all got our discs and we popped them in, and most of us won nothing, but lo and behold, when Paddy Ryan, owner of the Ardilaun

Hotel, popped his in, he hit the jackpot! He won £1,800, which was a fortune at the time, and we had a great night on the proceeds.

All of this talk of Switzerland and Austria reminds me of another story that's not strictly travel related, but that involves me playing host to 100 Swiss people in Kerry, all of whom were determined to have a good time ...

It began when I was doing sales calls in Munich and I was on my way back to my hotel after my day's work. I am always on the lookout for a new sales opportunity, and when I spotted the office of a major travel agent, I saw my chance. In I went and I explained that I was a hotelier from Ireland and asked if I could talk to someone. Luckily, the woman in charge of the whole group was there and she was delighted to talk to me. Maria was her name, I recall, and we chatted away for a bit, before she said, 'Tell me, do you do anything different?'

I said, 'Well, we do picnics in the Black Valley. We go on horseback and have lunch outside Lord Brandon's Cottage, then we go back down the lakes on a boat. It's a full day, but it's fantastic.' Those of you who know the Black Valley, in the middle of Killarney National Park, will know what I mean. 'Very interesting,' she said, and we said our goodbyes.

That summer, I heard not a word, nor the summer after, but two years later, I got a phone call. 'Hello! Are you the hotel that does tents near the park in Kenmare?'

'Tents near the park in Kenmare?' That had me scratching my head for a bit, before the penny dropped. 'Oh, are you Maria, the girl from Germany?'

Yes, she was, she told me, and I had to tell her that we didn't do tents in the park in Kenmare, but we could do anything, I supposed, within reason.

'Well,' she replied, 'I have a plan to discuss with you.' She went on to explain that she had two groups of 50 people who were looking for a special outward-bound experience for two weekends in October. They were Swiss and from the soup company Maggi, and the weekend was a reward for good sales. Maria wanted them to spend a night out in the open – in tents – and then another night in the hotel.

'No trouble,' I said, thinking, oh, Lord where do I start? I decided to begin with the tents. I knew that I couldn't go to a camping shop and ask for a 50-person tent, so I went to the local Civil Defence and they helped me to set up a camp in the National Park. It wasn't a dry night, of course, but I'd got hold of a huge parachute – don't ask me where – and we'd strung it on a pole over the camp, so it was waterproof. So far, so good, but they had to fish for their breakfast the next day and I knew there wouldn't be fish at that time of the year, so I went to a trout farm in West Cork and we bought 100 trout from them. We kept them in drums up the river and just before the Maggi city slickers went fishing, we tossed them in around the corner. I know, we were breaking every rule in the book, but the Maggis caught a good few and were very happy.

The local park ranger was less so, understandably enough. He popped in to see me at work. 'What are you doing with the fish?'

I said, 'I'm putting them in the river.'

'Oh, no, you can't do that, Francis.' I was aware of the fact that these were farmed and that what we were doing wasn't strictly right, but the problem wasn't actually that. It was that the season had closed on 30 September and this was 4 October!

Fair enough, I thought. We decided then to do skeet or clay-pigeon shooting in lieu of the fishing the next weekend, and we set it all up, with local experts. The shoot began and the Maggis were having a great time taking cracks at the clay-pigeon tiles, and I was congratulating myself on a job well done, when I heard a roar behind me. Next thing, I saw the park ranger running across the field, trousers hanging off him as he tried to tie his belt. He lived in a cottage in the park and the racket had woken him up and he'd come running out into the park. 'For God's sake, what are you doing?' he asked me when he caught up with me, breathless from running across the fields. 'Don't you know you're not allowed to shoot in a national park?'

'Listen,' I said. 'I have 50 Swiss people here and there'll be a riot if I try to stop them.'

Muttering and mumbling under his breath, he then told me to get them out of there as soon as they were finished and took off in the direction of home. He should have let me fish ... What I didn't tell the park ranger is that it was one of the most profitable visits of my career to date. I took £104,000 off our visitors, an extraordinary amount. And Maria paid me for the tents!

For the Birds

No tour of Europe would be complete without a visit to the United Kingdom, but of all the countries I've visited, I've probably spent the least time there. I don't have any UK-based relatives and most of my business dealings would be in the USA, so I have yet to experience that country in any great detail and all of my experiences are of the transport variety. I did push a vintage bus up The Mall once, during a conference in 1985. We'd been invited to a black-tie event to celebrate the launch of a guide to Ireland, and it was freezing, and there we all were in our monkey-suits, pushing a British Leyland bus up The Mall! I can also remember getting a taxi home after a very posh party at the Connaught Hotel, beloved of many an English gentleman, and being very disappointed, because my invitation had promised me 'carriages at midnight'. I'd fully expected a carriage to pull up outside the front door – imagine my disappointment.

Of course, no trip to England would be complete without a transport story; my good friend Frank shared one with me recently. He went to a train station in a regional city – we won't shame it! – and wanted a train to London. No big deal, you might think, so he queued up at the ticket booth and when his turn came, he said, 'I'd like a single ticket to London for tomorrow, please.'

'Oh, I'm afraid you can't have one of those,' the man behind the counter said.

'Why not?' Frank was incredulous – where else would he be getting a single ticket to London, except in a train station?

'Because the fellow who issues the London tickets is sick today. And he'll be sick tomorrow too.'

Things were getting stranger by the minute, Frank thought. 'How do I get a ticket to London, then?'

'You can get one tomorrow from the ticket machine on the platform.'

'But what happens if I want to reserve a seat?' Frank asked, not unreasonably.

'Oh, you won't have a problem, there are loads of seats on that train.'

It made sense, Frank thought, in the surreal world he had now entered. He sighed, 'Fine, so what do I do then?'

'You turn up tomorrow and get a ticket.'

So he did and he saved £2 into the bargain!

I also, like a real tourist eejit, got stuck on a Tube in London once, which frightened the life out of me. I was going into town from Heathrow with a colleague, John Prendiville, from The Waterville Lake Hotel. The two of us had got the Tube and were to change in Piccadilly. We were in a rush, because it was nearly five o'clock and we were supposed to be at the venue then, so even though the Tube was full when it pulled in, we squeezed on. Of course, I couldn't get in properly, so, when the door shut, I ended up with my briefcase, and my arm from my elbow down, sticking out of the carriage. Normally, the doors open if there's an obstruction, so I waited for a few seconds, but nothing happened. I wasn't in pain, but I would have liked my arm back! I wriggled my arm a bit and my fellow passengers tried to prise the door open, to no avail.

And then the train started moving down the platform, gathering speed as it headed towards the tunnel. Sacred Heart, I thought, I'm a goner.

So, there we were, zooming down the platform, and I was beginning to panic. I was worried that when I got to the tunnel, I might bash my lovely briefcase off the wall – how I wasn't worried about losing an arm, I don't know ... Suddenly, my eye caught that of a man wearing a bowler hat and carrying an umbrella. He nodded to me as if exchanging a secret signal, whereupon I dropped the suitcase and he picked it up. My arm was still sticking out, but no sooner had I dropped the suitcase onto the platform than the train stopped. The door opened and I got out, walking down the platform to the bowler-hatted man. 'I had it for you. Best of luck,' he said, in that British way, as if nothing at all had happened. I thanked him, took the briefcase from him, got into the waiting train and off we went, without another word! We got to our show in time, by the way, but I am always very cautious getting on public transport now.

However, my favourite English story involves twitchers on the Scilly Isles. Bear with me! Every year, we at the Park Hotel Kenmare take a staff holiday during the closed season, generally in January, and one year, we chose the Scilly Isles. I have no idea why: I suspect it was because we thought it would be a tiny bit warmer than Kerry in the wintertime. In fact, the two places have quite similar microclimates. The Scilly Isles are about 45 kilometres south-west of Cornwall, and are famous for their flowers, because of their sub-tropical climate.

Because the islands are on the Gulf Stream, the water is turquoise and the soil warm, so they can grow just about everything. When we were there, the daffodils were out – in the depths of winter. In fact, that's one of the main attractions of the Scilly Isles: the exotic planting. The highlight of a garden visit will be Tresco Abbey Gardens, a 19th-century garden planted by a man called Augustus Smith, who developed the garden as his own private hideaway on the grounds of an old abbey. Today the gardens are full to bursting with exotic plants and trees, all sheltered from the Atlantic by walls and hedges. Tresco Abbey is also where you can see figureheads that have been discovered from old shipwrecks, if that's your thing!

There are a great many little islands, but only five of them are inhabited, so it's very unspoiled with lovely sandy beaches and lots of wildlife. Birdwatching is a real thing on the Scilly Isles, as you can imagine, and they take it ever so seriously.

Anyway, my friend Liz O'Mahony and I decided to take a little reconnaissance trip to the isles to see if they might work for a staff holiday. We ended up on St Martin's, a lovely island with fabulous beaches and lots of wildlife, and we were going to head to one of the smaller islands where people go to watch birds – hence the twitchers! We were sitting on the pier waiting for our boat when the birdwatchers began to arrive. They were like a flock of birds themselves, all dressed identically in camouflage, dark brown shoes and with their sandwiches in tinfoil, huge sets of binoculars around their necks. They all looked highly serious and didn't speak to each other, and of course, Liz and I got a fit of the giggles watching them all flock together on the pier. The more they kept coming, the more Liz and I had the giggles – it was like being in church. It might sound a bit childish and we weren't laughing at these people, I hasten to add, but at the strangeness of the whole thing, with herself and myself in our bright summer clothes, sitting in the middle of brown and green. Every time Liz looked at me, we'd collapse. They must have thought we'd had a big row, because the tears were rolling down her face.

After all of that, we did go to the Scilly Isles for our staff holidays and had a most wonderful trip – it was actually one of the best staff holidays we've had. We started on Polurrian on the Lizard Peninsula, where we stayed for two nights in a local hotel. The owner, a Mr Francis, was a lovely man, delighted to do things with a big gang of enthusiastic Irish people. He arranged this big dinner for us and the entertainment was provided by an English travelling troupe who performed extracts from Chaucer's *Canterbury Tales.* Let's just say, they might be about pilgrims to Canterbury, but they are very bawdy. The language out of them was choice, but it was allowed given the context. I was a lord for the night and I was only delighted, even if I had to kiss one of the actors' feet. It was a great success, but the next day's visit to a stately home was a bit less so: the staff got the giggles as the owner, a very nice lady with marbles in her mouth, showed us around. It must have been catching ...

A highlight of our visit was taking one of those huge helicopters like a Sikorsky from Cornwall to the Scilly Isles. It was really something else to clamber on board the huge helicopter. Interesting transport was to be something of a theme on this holiday: we took a World War II landing craft for a treasure hunt with a difference on St Martin's. I can still remember it was freezing cold, but sunny, with bright blue skies and white clouds. We took off in our landing craft, charging for the beach. We had to be ready for the front to drop and for us all to run onto the sand. Now, the staff had stayed up late as they always do on holiday, determined to enjoy themselves, so I'm not sure if they'd slept, but they didn't know what hit them. Water was pouring into the boat and Liz piped up, 'Where am I?' I could see her thinking, how have I ended up in the Normandy landings?! The organisers had found big rounded stones and marked them with an 'x' and we had to find them, which wasn't easy as they were all over the island and the clues were encrypted. We exhausted ourselves running all over the place, which probably woke some of the gang up! It was a fantastic holiday and the staff have never forgotten it, nor the last day's event, a Gaelic football and cricket event. The island people turned out in force to play a football match against us and in return, we played cricket against them. Most of us had never seen a cricket bat in our lives, except for yours truly, who had played in CUS in my lovely cricket whites.

Many years later, one of my staff, Peggy O'Connor, who worked in the stillroom, as we call it, where you make sandwiches, tea and toast, etc., said to me, 'You know, Mr Brennan, only for you, I would have gone nowhere in the world.' I'm not saying this to show off, but to add that I was only delighted to be able to give the staff a bit of fun. We all work very hard at the hotel and we're a real team, and we all deserve a break every now and then. That's the whole point of travel, I feel, not just to tick things off on a to-do list, but to spend time with the people who matter to us. So, while I might be a fan of more exotic places, Europe is special to me because of the time I've spent there with other people. As Ernest Hemingway put it: 'Never go on trips with anyone you do not love.'

MOROCCO
Marrakesh
Atlas Mountains
Capernaum
Tel Aviv
Jerusalem
Cairo
EGYPT
Luxor
The Nile
Emi Koussi
CHAD
Lalibela
ETHIOPIA
KENYA
Nairobi
N
W
E
S
Johannesburg
Lesotho
Robben Island
SOUTH AFRICA
Durban
East London
Kenton-On-Sea
Cape Town

From Suez to Cape Horn: Africa and the Middle East

'One's destination is never a place,
but rather a new way
of looking at things.'

Henry Miller

I have left Africa until last in this book, not because I haven't enjoyed my trips there, but probably because this is the one part of the world that remains a bit of a mystery to me. We're inclined, when we think of Africa, to see it as one big country, but my travels there, limited as they might have been, have made me realise that this isn't true at all. There is a world of difference between the north of the continent and the people who live there, and the south, as I've learned from my trips to Morocco and Egypt, and then Kenya and Ethiopia and, finally, South Africa. I've barely scratched the surface, but I've found Africa to be a lot more complex and diverse than I'd imagined. My research tells me that it has one of the oldest civilisations, with the Ancient Egyptians, the greatest amount of natural resources, including 40 per cent of the world's gold, and the largest number of languages, with 2,000 different languages spoken on the continent. Also, the continent is home to 99 per cent of the world's lion population, and species like the hippo and gorilla can only be found in Africa, according to *National Geographic* magazine. Imagine if we had all that in Europe!

North Africa is separated from the rest of the continent by the Sahara Desert. I'm sure you all know that, but did you also know that the Sahara is 9.4 million square kilometres in size? You can't say that I'm not teaching you anything in this book! The desert isn't just sand, either: it has mountain ranges in it, with the highest peak being Chad's Emi Koussi, at 3,415 metres, and it's home to animals like the deathstalker scorpion, which sounds terrifying, as well as the desert fox and a whole range of creepy-crawlies. I had no idea anything could survive in that heat, but it does.

I haven't been into the Sahara proper, but I have skirted it a couple of times. I was travelling with my friend Mary Bowe of Marlfield House Hotel after a Relais and Châteaux (another hotel organisation) congress and we decided to go on a tour of the Atlas Mountains. And it was. The Atlas Mountains cover a large part of Morocco, as well as Algeria and Tunisia. We were guests of the Berber people, a tribe who originally roamed throughout the area and are known for their skill in navigating the Sahara. They were in North Africa before the Arabs arrived, and they saw off the Romans and the French, which is some record. They have their own language, which has survived all of the invasions, and their own culture and customs. They also have their own crafts in silver and pewter and seeing this tradition in action was fascinating.

After a few days, we took a taxi down from the mountains into Marrakech. I was a bit surprised to see a Renault car with 'Taxi' written on a sign on the top, in the middle of the mountains – it would be like finding a taxi at the foot of Carrauntoohil! But one of the locals explained to me that there were lots of taxis in places you might not expect in Morocco, because at the time, public transport was limited. The other thing we hadn't realised is that taxis are all shared, and as we sat in the back of the car chatting to the driver in a mixture of bad French and English, people began to hop in beside us. As he drove along, he would stop every now and then, and someone new would get in, nodding and chatting away before stopping seemingly in the middle of nowhere, pressing a coin into his hand and waving goodbye. It was all a bit bewildering, but we arrived in Marrakech happy as Larry.

Marrakech is a lovely city and it was as exotic and glamorous as I'd expected. It was a big draw for artists during the 1960s, and people like Jimi Hendrix and the Rolling Stones were frequent visitors. The Djemaa el-Fna is the epicentre of the city, a huge square full of market stalls and bustling with life at all hours of the day and night. It began life as a place where you went to see public executions, but thankfully they have been replaced by nicer entertainments, such as acrobats, food stalls and crafts. It really does have a mediaeval feel to it though, with all of the acts and the bustle and the firelight. And the souk is out of this world, a huge warren of little streets filled with stalls, selling everything from jewellery to leather to herbal remedies and more.

Yves Saint Laurent's home was a must-see for me in Marrakech. There's a museum now, but then it was a villa and garden called the Jardin Majorelle, famous for its electric-blue building and amazing gardens. YSL bought it having discovered Marrakech in the late 1960s and he and his partner maintained the gardens. When he died, he left it to the city; the new museum has displays of his fashion and sketches, and the museum's director said that the designer took a lot of inspiration from local people, particularly from brightly coloured Berber clothing. Sadly, I don't own any Yves Saint Laurent, unless you count a couple of ties.

Another iconic place in Marrakech is the Mamounia Hotel, once the home of Prince Mamoun and now a luxury hotel, with fantastic views of the Koutoubia Minaret and the city as a whole. It was a favourite of Winston Churchill and they have named a bar after him. It's very sumptuous but I know lots of people who just come to the gardens for a cocktail to get the spirit of the place without needing to pay for a night's accommodation – fair enough!

At that time in Morocco, transport in general was quite entertaining: we took a bus one day to the seaside town of Essaouira, a very pretty fortified town on the west coast of the country that is a favourite with kitesurfers. It blows a gale all year round here, keeping mass tourism at bay, which makes it such a nice experience just to wander around the town. It has a lovely medina and according to UNESCO, who made it a World Heritage Site, it is 'an outstanding and well-preserved example of a mid-18th century fortified seaport town, with a strong European influence translated to a North African context'. What I found interesting when I visited was that haggling wasn't the done thing, unlike in other parts of the country. After a week or two in the country, I had got used to bargaining – in fact, I was even beginning to enjoy myself – but there was no haggling in Essaouira. I marched into a shop that made lovely wooden boxes and picked one up, read the price sticker on the back and approached the man behind the counter. 'How much is this?' I asked.

'The price is on the sticker,' he said, looking at me as if I was half mad.

'Oh. Well, will you take a hundred and fifty for it?' I persisted, like an eejit. (The currency in Morocco is the dirham and one is equal to about nine cent.)

'These are handmade and the price is the price,' he said politely. Finally, the penny dropped, so I handed over the correct price and got a lovely wooden box that I still have to this day.

It was the transport, though, that made it worthwhile, as we boarded a very old Bedford bus full to bursting with local people: there were so many that they had to pull little stools out from under the seats for people to sit on. It was obviously a regular occurrence, but I couldn't believe that there wasn't a health and safety issue due to the numbers. Sure enough, when the driver saw a police patrol at one point on the road, he let a big shout out of him – 'Police!' – and everybody ducked so they wouldn't be spotted!

People of the Black Land

I loved the colour and life in Morocco, but in terms of variety of landscape and history, Egypt is really the place, and the title above refers to the name the Ancient Egyptians gave to their country. In 1986, a few friends and myself decided we'd make our dream of going down the Nile a reality – fine, you might think, but this was the year Gaddafi's Libya was bombed by the USA and there were only 29 of us on a boat designed to take hundreds. The only people who weren't Irish were a couple of French people, who seemed to enjoy all the craic.

We began in Luxor, the ancient capital of the pharaohs, and home to the Valley of the Kings, which, as you can imagine, was out of this world. There are more than 60 tombs in the valley, containing the remains of Egypt's pharaohs from the New Kingdom, about 1500–1000 BC. The most famous is King Tutankhamun, of course, discovered by Howard Carter in 1922. The tombs were fascinating and their history even more so: they were packed with all the things the nobility might need in the afterlife, from gold and silver to furniture, food and drink – in case they might get hungry on the way! I also found it interesting to learn that when the kings were mummified, their organs were all taken out and carefully preserved, all except their brains, which were thrown away. When I read up about it, I found an historian, Joyce Tyldesley, who explained that the Egyptians believed that your intelligence lay in your heart, not your head. Maybe the Egyptians knew something we didn't!

After a fancy dress evening where we all donned various Egyptian-style outfits, including a priest who dressed up as the Pharoah, we continued to Aswan, a lovely city from where you can take one of the famous feluccas downriver. We took one at sunset and it was so lovely and old-worldly as we floated along in one of the traditional sailing boats – not unlike a Galway Hooker. While in Aswan, we were told to visit the temples of Abu Simbel, on the border with Sudan, but it was a bit too far, which is a pity, because when I've seen photographs of them since, they are extraordinary: you'd think in a country coming down with fantastic temples that you might not be impressed, but these four statues of Ramesses II are carved out of a cliff and are 66 feet high. Interestingly, I read that the Egyptians aligned the temple so that the sun would illuminate them at certain times of the year, just like Newgrange here.

We did get to the grave of the Aga Khan in Aswan, however. It's beautiful and very serene, even if one of the party had a bit of a catastrophe there. It began with our evening camel ride up the mountain to the grave. I've gone on camels a few times, so I'm used to them, in particular to getting off one, which is a two-stage process. Camels drop on their knees, then on their hips, so there are two big bumps that you have to look out for. If you're not paying attention, you can think the camel is finished after one bump and go to get off, but if you do, you'll get a nasty bounce and fall off. One of our party, a man from Mayo, wasn't paying attention to the double bounce; when we came down the mountain after our trip, I reminded him by shouting, 'Be careful,' but when the camel dropped once, he went to jump off. Too late – the camel sat down on his hips with a big bump and my friend slid down the neck of the camel and, let's just say, injured his 'town halls'. You might think this funny, but he sustained a serious injury. The poor man took months to recover and needed an operation. The camel wasn't very happy either!

After our fantastic cruise, we returned to Cairo and we were then flying to Tel Aviv to see some of the Holy Land, until we discovered that our flight was cancelled. There was ferocious bedlam altogether because EgyptAir had cancelled our booking – just because. There was no explanation. Now to get from Egypt to Israel wasn't easy, in spite of the countries being next door to each other – for political reasons, I suppose – so there was no way I wanted to miss this flight. Besides, everything was booked and confirmed, so it was time to take on the airline representative. When I went to the man behind the desk, he protested that we hadn't paid. I was persistent, but he wasn't having any of it, even though I knew full well we'd paid. Then I had a brainwave. 'Well, could we pay again?'

The man disappeared into an office and came back with a sheaf of forms. 'Sign these,' he commanded. We had no clue what they were, but we signed! To this day, I have never been asked for a penny by EgyptAir, which is nice of them.

Before heading to Tel Aviv, we went into Cairo and saw all of the museums and marvelled at the treasures and the Pyramids of Giza, of course, before heading back to our hotel. I can still remember that the bus driver went at 120 miles an hour and I thought, Holy God, if we bump into a cat, we'll all be killed. And the traffic was unbelievable.

Cairo is known as the 'City of a Thousand Minarets', because of the huge number of mosques, and I was dying to see inside one, so a few of us set off. We were just going out of the revolving door of the hotel when who should be coming in only a great friend of mine, Brendan Winkle from San Francisco, who organised tours of the Middle East via Travcoa, a big high-end travel company. He was delighted to see me and happily told me how to get to the mosque, so off we all went.

When we arrived, we had to take off our shoes, of course, and put them into little boxes. The mosque was huge and full of people saying prayers. In the centre of the building was a huge door and lots of people were heading towards it and I said, 'I wonder what's going on in there?' Sometimes, my curiosity gets the better of me! We went over respectfully and moseyed along, only to find ourselves swept along down the corridor in a mass of people. Suddenly, I noticed that I was by myself in this moving mass of people and I could see policemen on a plinth with guns, moving people along. Oh, my God, I thought, what's going on here? However, I didn't have much choice but to continue, because the mass of people kept moving and they were all waving their hands in the air. Much later, I learned that the mosque was home to an edition of the original Koran and people wanted to touch the container holding the sacred book. I kept getting belted on the head as people reached over me to touch the box! It was so hot and crowded and such a squash as we headed past the Koran and down another corridor, until finally I was squeezed out into a quiet place – it was like being born again. Of course, the rest of my friends popped out then, giving out stink to me for getting us involved in the melee. Worse, we'd come out in a different place to where we'd come in, so we had to locate our shoes – and we had no notion where they were. All I kept thinking was that no-one would want my odd-sized shoes! I couldn't imagine them being desired by an Egyptian. We went outside the mosque to get our bearings and had to do a full circuit in our bare feet before locating our shoes once more.

Ancient History

Removing items of clothing reminds me of my trip to Jerusalem following our trip to Tel Aviv, when I was required to drop my pants ... read on! We were at the Skål conference in Jerusalem and we took a day trip up to the Sea of Galilee, which many of you will know as the place where Jesus performed many miracles. It felt very emotional to be sitting by the side of the lake which we knew from our readings of the New Testament in school and to imagine miracles like Jesus walking on water, and the catch of fish, when Jesus asked Peter to lower his nets into the water. Peter protested, because they had all come up empty, but Jesus insisted and of course, when he pulled the nets in, he had a huge catch. Coincidentally, we were offered a lunch of lovely barbecued fish when we were there, all 600 of us, which we were told was 'St Peter's fish'. I later discovered that it was tilapia and apparently the lake had to be restocked a few years ago, because it had almost disappeared due to all the hungry eaters.

There's a monastery there on the site where Jesus performed the miracle of the Loaves and the Fishes – where he managed to feed the 5,000, if you recall – called Tabgha. When we visited, it was occupied by nuns. Of course we wanted to have a look, but I was wearing shorts, and when we walked in through the gate, this elderly nun approached and pointed at me. 'No, no, you can't come in in shorts – long trousers or to the knee only,' she said crossly.

Now, my shorts came half-way down my thigh – picture that, if you will – so they were clearly no good. My friend Mary begged the nun to relent, but she refused, shaking her head then turning on her heel and disappearing into the monastery. I went back outside to wait, my tail between my legs, when a young nun passed me.

'What brings you out here?' she asked.

'I'm not allowed in,' I said.

'Why not?'

'Because I'm in shorts.'

'Oh, for God's sake. Just take the belt off and drop them.'

'Drop my pants?' I said, open-mouthed. I thought I was hearing things.

'Just loosen the belt and lower your shorts a bit and they'll be fine.' This was long before rap artists got the idea of showing off their underpants, so the nun was clearly ahead of her time. I went into the House of God, trousers dropped, and the older nun was none the wiser.

Capernaum is a little bit further along the Sea of Galilee, and is another important site of a number of Jesus's miracles. In Capernaum, the Gospel tells us, he healed a number of people, including a man who was lowered through the ceiling of the temple on a stretcher. Capernaum is also home to one of the oldest synagogues in the world, and here we all were, 600 of us from all over the world, walking around in history. Mind you, because these sites are so popular, the locals aren't afraid to 'monetise' them, to use the popular term!

(Speaking of this, I got a terrible fright in Jerusalem at the Holy Sepulchre. This is one of the most important places for Christians to visit, as it's home to the grave and crucifixion site of Our Lord. As so many Christian communities want to visit, the key to the church is minded by a Muslim family, by ancient decree, and another Muslim family opens the door to the Holy Sepulchre every morning, which I think is very ecumenical. As you can imagine, the site is full of history, having been built, destroyed and rebuilt many times over the centuries. There is a magnificent gold altar in the church called the Altar of the Crucifixion, where you can see the Rock of Calvary, where Jesus died, in a glass case, so you can imagine how precious the place is to so many communities. The tomb of Our

Lord is the centrepiece of the visit and when I was there, there was a very long queue. It has since been restored and there's a very nice mausoleum called the Edicule over the grave, but as far as I can remember, we just bent down and shuffled into a tiny dark cave. Next thing, a hand shot out and a box was rattled in my face! There was no way of escaping and no-one could move without stuffing something into the box, so we could have been putting in anything at all.)

Back at the Sea of Galilee, when we had soaked it all up, the many buses that had been hired to take us back to Jerusalem appeared and we all clambered on. Now, I'm a bit of a control freak when I'm on these tours, I'll freely admit, so when our bus turned left instead of right at the end of the road, I said to the lady in charge of our tour, 'We should be going right, why are we turning left? Are we going north? I think we should be going south.'

'Sit right back down,' she barked. 'Who do you think you are?' She gave me a right bashing in front of the whole bus. I was mortified, but sat back down like a good boy. Anyway, the Irish bus is considered to be the most desirable to be on, because we always have fun, a sing-song, and a bit of craic. This time, we decided to play charades and each person would have to go up to the front of the bus and do a charade – the tour lady really loved that! She kept telling us to sit down, but we invited her to join in, which didn't amuse her.

I'd forgotten all about going the wrong way until, half an hour later, we went through a chicane of oil barrels, which were on fire, and then we screeched to a halt in front of a roadblock. Suddenly, we were surrounded by a lot of men with big guns. It turned out that we were up at the Golan Heights, two hours north of where we should have been, and what's more, we were at a Palestinian checkpoint. There was a bit of frantic explaining on the tour guide's part, a rapid reverse turn and a drive all the way back, passing Capernaum once more, before arriving back in Jerusalem, three hours behind schedule. All the ladies were frantic as it was the President's dinner night and they were missing their hair appointments – but it was worth it for the unscheduled bit of excitement, as well as a reminder that where we were was a divided place, where very different people have to live on top of each other.

Sub-Saharan Africa

The Africa south of the Sahara Desert is a completely different place to those countries that border the Mediterranean. Of course, we probably associate that sea with all of the waves of migrants crossing it nowadays, and it's true to say that many of them come from sub-Saharan Africa, looking for a better life in Europe and, in many cases, fleeing wars. Watching the news recently, I was reminded of my 2010 trip to Ethiopia, a country which really has remained with me in so many ways.

Brody Sweeney is a businessman who made his name with O'Brien's sandwich bars and whom I've known for a long time. He called me one day and said he'd like to have a meeting with me. He was involved with an organisation called Connect Ethiopia that built trade links directly with the country and he wanted to talk to me about a very interesting project to improve tourism in Lalibela in northern Ethiopia. If you haven't heard of Lalibela – and I hadn't – it's a fascinating place and one that really deserves tourism.

It's best known for its stunning churches, all cut out of the rock face, built by Coptic Christians in the 13th and 14th centuries on the instructions of King Lalibela. These churches are truly extraordinary, built down into the rocks, or under the ground, all connected by little tunnels. You don't even see them until you're upon them. I can still remember one of them, St George's Church, being a simple cross in the ground, but when you came closer, you looked down to see a full church below you. Biete Medhane Alem is probably the most impressive church; it resembles a Greek temple, and you can imagine the skill it took to build it. It is also home to the Lalibela Cross, a very ornate gold cross which is used in blessings and ceremonies. The cross was stolen at one point and found its way to a dealer in Belgium, before being returned to its home. *Vogue* magazine declared Lalibela 'the next Machu Picchu', which is really something, and well deserved, but I'd hope it wouldn't get quite that busy.

The idea was that a few of us would go out to Lalibela and talk to the locals about bringing more visitors to their town. So Kevin Thornton did a restaurant course with them; Jack Crotty, another food entrepreneur, came too and worked with a local farm to develop farm visits; I was working with hotel people and my job was to talk to local students at a catering college about greeting and reception skills; and I brought a friend of mine, Bridget O'Connell, to talk about accommodation. Our aim was to leave the tourism industry there with better trained staff and some tourist infrastructure, such as a village experience, a mountain trail, transport to a walk with lunch and so on, plus ideas for creating new jobs and revenue. The locals in the town were keen to get people to stay longer in the area rather than only visiting the churches, which would be the main draw, of course, and rightly so.

There was only one small problem for some of us. Lalibela is at a high altitude, about 8,500 feet above sea level, so sickness can be an issue and sadly, Bridget didn't feel well at all. It turned out that she had altitude sickness, which leads to thickening of the blood and can be very dangerous, so she had to return to Addis Ababa. I thought you only got it going up Everest, but I learned something new! Bridget was absolutely fine once she returned to a lower altitude.

We have a few preconceptions of Ethiopia in Ireland, such as about the levels of hunger. Of course, while I didn't see starvation in Lalibela, a great many were hungry elsewhere. What I also didn't know but now do, thanks to the *Ethiopian Herald*, is that a huge number of people have flooded into Ethiopia because of wars elsewhere – about 850,000 of them, which is a lot for a country that isn't wealthy. However, I don't think I'd realised how many fabulous historical places there would be there, perhaps because Ethiopia was one of two African countries not to have been colonised long-term by Europeans (the other is Liberia, for you general-knowledge fans). The Ethiopians are a lovely people and mad to learn: I used to see the children going to school every morning in their immaculate school uniforms while I was there. I forged a nice friendship with a man called Solomon Jerusalem, a fellow hotelier who came to stay with me in the Park, and who still writes to me to this day.

'Jambo'

This means 'hello' in Swahili, the national language of Kenya. It's just south of Ethiopia, but it's a very different place. It's a country I've visited a few times and I love the culture and energy of the place. My first trip was for a Skål conference in 1984 and I can still remember a funny story about the hotel in Nairobi. When we checked into the hotel, one of my friends, Mary Bennett, asked for the loan of my travel hairdryer (I would have one, wouldn't I?!). Of course she could have it, I said.

Now, as a singleton, you generally get the worst room in the house and it doesn't bother me at all – I'm used to it at this stage – so, when a young lad arrived in reception to show me to my room, I didn't think anything of it. He took my bag and led me out of the front door, down through the garden, out through a gate, across a field, left again down a lane. Where in the name of God are we going, I wondered. I'm miles away from the hotel. Finally, after my little trip into the countryside, we arrived at another, smaller building and I was shown my room. I'd say it was the staff quarters, or an annex of some kind.

I was filthy because we'd travelled in open-topped Westfalia buses through the game reserve from a village we'd visited earlier. I hopped into the shower and switched it on and dirty black water began to pour down me. Oh my God, I thought, this water is filthy, but it was better than nothing, I told myself, trying to scrub myself clean as best I could. The phone rang then, so I put a towel around me and ran to get it.

'Good afternoon,' the voice said, 'Is that Francis Brennan?'

'It is,' I replied, wondering what this could be about.

'This is the general manager of the hotel. You've been given the wrong room, so I'm coming to get you.'

That's strange, I thought, but as I was talking to him, a ton of dirt was streaking down my chest and arm. 'Can you give me 20 minutes?' I asked him. 'I've actually just stepped out of the shower.'

'Oh, that's fine,' he replied.

I went back to the shower and turned on the water and thought, my God, I'll never get clean, as dirt streamed off me. Then I realised it wasn't the water that was dirty, it was me! My head was caked in henna dust from the journey. I laughed away at my own stupidity and stood under the water until finally it ran clean. I got myself organised and the boy came back for me and we recommenced our journey, down the hill, over the road, through the gate, past the field and so on, until we reached a lovely, lush garden. I was shown to a very nicely appointed garden room, quite an upgrade from the staff quarters! I looked forward to telling the gang at dinner time that I'd been upgraded to a suite with a garden view, bedroom and lounge.

When I went downstairs later on, I boasted of my lovely new room.

'Oh, I know what's happened,' said Mary Bennett. 'I borrowed your hair dryer and then I put it down and I couldn't remember where it was. I was running around the front hall like a lunatic going, "Where did I put it?" and one of the staff noticed and asked me what was wrong. "Oh, I'm after losing the hairdryer of Francis Brennan and he's the best hotelier in Ireland and he'll kill me."'

The man went back to the office and looked at his list and noticed, to his horror, that the 'best hotelier in Ireland' had been dumped into the staff quarters – he had to reverse me out of there and that's how I got the good room!

Rested from my good night's sleep in the best room in the hotel, I set off with the gang for a Maasai village the next day. I had read up a bit on the Maasai and their semi-nomadic way of life, herding their cattle across the savannah, and I'd seen photos of their bright-red-and-purple clothing and intricate beadwork, and I was dying to know more. Even so, I was a bit wary, to be honest, as some village experiences can be a bit phony, so I probed the tour operator a bit. I was anxious to see a proper village: I didn't want to see the Bunratty of Kenya. I wanted to see the real thing. The operator explained to me, 'That's not normally done, because they're very shy and don't want photographs.' (This was a few years ago. Now, many Maasai offer village experiences as a way of supplementing their income.)

'Well, we'll leave the cameras, then,' I volunteered, 'and we'll be very respectful and quiet.'

It was agreed and so we arrived at the village that was off the beaten track and wouldn't have seen tourists. Before we got off the bus, I gave the gang a pep talk. After all, we'd landed in on the local Maasai people and they weren't expecting us. I had told everyone 'no cameras' – in the days when there were real cameras – and I had read that if they put a bracelet on you, it is understood that you have to buy it. 'Now, listen, gang, don't put bracelets on unless you plan to keep them, and no photos,' I reminded them.

The village was a compound in a huge circle with a fence all around it to keep the animals out. Even though the Maasai have their own herds of cattle and goats, they have a lot of trouble from wild animals, so they've developed ingenious ways of dealing with them. For example, the houses are all round, and when you open the front door, you enter a circular corridor that you follow all the way inside. The reason for this is that an animal won't go around a circle because it thinks it'll never get out – it's a simple, clever design.

The Maasai very kindly agreed to let me and Mary look inside one of their houses, and we were shown into a large circular room, divided into living and bedroom space, where they burned elephant dung to keep the mosquitoes away – very effective, if smelly. I found the smoke from the fire a bit eye-watering, but of course, they were used to it.

I made a great friend at the Maasai village, a man who looked ageless and very dignified in his red robes and beaded jewellery. I was also very impressed with his novel way of extending the hole in his earlobe –

it's a tradition – with three Kodak 35mm plastic film containers. Very effective!

My new friend chatted to me all the way around the village, and when we were leaving, he pointed to my runners and asked if I'd be interested in swapping with him. He had some very nice leather sandals, but as the Maasai are very tall as a rule, well over six feet, they have feet to match – the sandals would be swimming on me! Besides, I thought, of all the people in the world, you don't want my different-sized shoes. 'I'll give you a dollar,' he offered.

'Look, let me explain.' I put my two heels together and showed him that I was wearing two shoes of different sizes. He was mystified, walking around me as if it was a magic trick, then he roared out to the rest and they all came to have a look, crowding around me. While this was going on, I looked up the village to see one of the gang, hands outstretched like Our Lord, with 100 bracelets on them. I thought, why on earth didn't you listen to me? Now, how are we going to get out of this? Next thing, I saw the Maasai coming towards me, necks stretched, spears at the ready, and they started jumping and singing. I'm not sure if you've ever seen the Maasai jump, but they can go feet in the air. It was entertaining, but I wondered if this was sinister in any way: we weren't even supposed to be in the village, and there we were, wandering around the houses, helping ourselves to bracelets ... It turned out that they were just showing us some of their traditional dance, and it was most impressive, even if we did have to bargain them down on the bracelets. I seem to recall that we gave them packs of cigarettes in exchange for them, after which I ushered the gang onto the bus before they could do any more damage! To this day, I am grateful to the Maasai for their hospitality and warmth – it reminded me in many ways of home years ago, where people would just call to the door and would be invited in for tea and biscuits.

We returned to Nairobi for the final evening of the conference, which was to be a dinner for the delegates and some local tourism officials. It was all very glam with everyone dressed up in their finery, and during the evening, some of the ladies met a man who told them that he was 'in precious stones'. He was a wholesaler for a large diamond supplier, he told them. At the time – and possibly still – it was considered a great way to move money, to buy diamonds with cash and take them with you to wherever you were going. I hasten to add that we bought ours from a legitimate wholesaler, like Weir's of Grafton Street, and I know that in those days, we weren't as aware of the ethical side of things as we are now. If you are buying gemstones, look for a reputable wholesaler who can tell you where the gems come from – or better still, buy a gemstone that's been 'grown' in a lab – apparently, you can't tell the difference, and that's because they imitate nature so well. A great idea, particularly if you are looking for something rare.

Anyway, the ladies arranged with him to go on Saturday to his shop and look at precious stones. On Friday there was lots of whispering, as they didn't want the husbands to know what they were up to, but yours truly was another matter. I was told that I had to come along!

I wasn't sure about the whole thing, but I thought I could offer a bit of protection if it all went south, to use gangster speak, so off we went into the city. The building where we were to meet our friend was well marked – in fact, there were lots of offices to do with stones and jewellery there – but even though we hung around for a bit, the gentleman didn't turn up.

'Are you sure you have the right place and the right time?' I said, walking down the corridor to see if there was anyone at home. Eventually, I reached a glass-panelled door and saw a man inside. I knocked and stuck my head around the door. 'Excuse me. Do you know if the gentleman is coming in today?'

The man looked up from his desk. 'Oh, he doesn't come in on a Saturday.'

'Well, I have five women here who are anxious to look at precious stones and they had an arrangement to meet him.'

'There are no stones in this building anyway,' he said, adding, 'You have to go to the warehouse. Would you like to come to mine? I'll get someone to come and collect you.' I hadn't a clue, but didn't want to disappoint the ladies, so I agreed, and went to wait in the corridor with them. Next thing, this gentleman appeared and said, 'Follow me.'

He looked very respectable, so off we went – nothing ventured! We went down onto the street, then up another street and down an alleyway and under washing hanging off lines and over open sewers. As we went further and further in, I began to feel a bit uneasy, wondering if this was a ruse and we'd be making the next day's newspaper headlines. Then we arrived at an industrial-type of building, the man knocked on a large door and a peephole opened. 'Joe sent me,' he said, and the security buzzer opened the door. This looks more promising, I thought, as the door closed behind us and we were faced with another door and another peephole. Surely this must be a place where they keep stones, I thought – otherwise why the security? He knocked on the door again and there was the same routine, then once more, before finally we went up a set of stairs and into a room with a table in it. Another man appeared and asked us what we were looking for. 'A selection,' I said, not sure what to say to make me sound like a professional.

'That's fine,' he said, leaving the room and returning a few moments later with a bucket in each hand. 'Excuse me,' he said, and emptied out two mounds, one on either end of the table, a pile of diamonds, emeralds, sapphires and tanzanite. We were gobsmacked.

'I'll leave you for half an hour and I'll come back when you've selected some,' he said happily. We could have shoved them into our pockets! He then explained that we'd need to root through the stones to find matching pairs and that one of the piles, the one with bigger stones, would make good matching necklaces and earrings.

'What about the cost?' I said.

'It's okay, we just price them according to their carat weight and you won't believe the price. Don't worry.'

The ladies dived into Aladdin's cave and started sorting through the stones, pulling little piles of them together. I was buying nothing, content to just admire them. I had no idea of their quality, but if the girls were happy, so was I. After a while, he came back in with his little weighing scales and weighed each of the girls' piles of stones. The value was unbelievable and I was tempted, I'll admit. I thought I should buy something and when I saw this little blue stone I slid it across the table. 'How much is that?'

The man took it in his tweezers and went to examine it and one of the girls piped up. 'Don't charge him too much – he's an orphan.' Me – an orphan?

'Oh, for an orphan,' he slid the stone back to me, 'There is no charge. It's with my compliments.' My friend gave me a kick under the table as I went to protest, and stones bought, we said our goodbyes and off we went. I couldn't believe it and wondered if it was some kind of Ocean's Eleven sting, but when we came home to Ireland every jeweller from Donegal to Cork said they were the best quality stones they'd seen and were terrific value. I now have a tanzanite tie-pin as a souvenir and I treasure it.

A Changing Country

I thought I'd end my African trip at the bottom – geographically! – with South Africa, because by the time you read this, I'll have returned from filming the new series of the *Grand Tour,* for which I was lucky enough to spend a fortnight with a great bunch of people in that country. I consider it a huge honour to be able to have adventures like this – a real privilege – and in such a spectacular setting. I've been to the country before, but every time I return, I'm reminded what an extraordinary place it is.

Strangely enough, a trip to the country in 2004 reminded me of home. I was at a conference in Durban, South Africa's third city and capital of KwaZulu-Natal. Durban has fantastic beaches and a nice tropical climate, because it's on South Africa's Indian Ocean coast. It's also home to a large Indian population, descended from workers who arrived in the province in the mid-19th century to work in the sugar plantations. Durban's most famous 'son' was Mahatma Gandhi. He wasn't born there, but he lived in the country for 20 years, having first travelled there as a young lawyer to help an Indian businessperson. It was here that he developed his ideas about peaceful protest, and this began when he was asked to leave a first-class carriage on a train, even though he had bought a ticket; when he refused, he was thrown off at Pietermaritzburg. Archbishop Desmond Tutu unveiled a statue to Gandhi in the city in 1993. Durban is also the home of Bunny Chow, which is a hollowed-out loaf of bread filled with curry, a local delicacy. No-one really knows how Bunny Chow evolved, but some think that filling a loaf with curry made it easier to transport to work on the plantations, which makes sense. I had to have Bunny Chow, of course, and even though I liked the curry, I wasn't so sure about the loaf of white bread!

When I talk of being reminded of home, though, I'm referring to my trip to Lesotho, which is a landlocked country in the eastern part of South Africa, about 300 kilometres from Durban. Lesotho has become quite a big issue in South Africa of late, because it has very few natural resources of its own, and many of the men have come to South Africa to work in the mines. It's very high up – most of it is nearly 6,000 feet above sea level, so the climate there is a complete contrast to tropical Durban.

We took off in a small bus, 12–14 of us, and I have never in my life seen roads like we saw, right on the edge of steep cliffs at a height of thousands of feet. I'm not joking! When I did some research on the roads in the country to jog my memory, I came across a website devoted entirely to dangerous roads (who knew such a thing existed?) and Lesotho had a great number of them. I can still remember clinging to the back of the seat in front of me as the bus chugged up a little road that zig-zagged up the side of a mountain, ending up at 10,500 feet above sea level at a place called the Tlaeeng Pass. What's more, because we were up so high, there was thunder and lightning and hailstones to beat the band. I have rarely been more terrified. If you'd like to visit the highest pub in Africa, by the way, you can do so at the Sani Pass, at a height of 9,436 feet.

We were visiting a mountain village, a cluster of round stone houses with thatched roofs. The residents don't need any protection here from wild animals, as unfortunately most of them have disappeared due to deforestation, apart from a bearded vulture which is described as 'magnificent'. When I went into one of the houses, I realised that the world is a small place, because it reminded me of my granny's home in Co. Sligo. My granny lived in a thatched cottage and cooked over an open fire with her three-legged pot: she used to make bread in it and she'd put the dough in, then place the lid on with coals on top. Now, here we were, thousands of miles away, and apart from the lino on the floor of this house, which would have been deluxe in my granny's time, the style of living here was exactly the same. The lady of the house had her pot and cooked on an open fire. She baked bread in exactly the same way, putting the coals on top, and I remember thinking, yes, many's the time I did that for Granny, and you'd have to replace the cold coals with hot ones to keep it all going. The lady showed us their animals and their little creamery and, again, it was so like Ireland 40 years before. It really brought me back and the nostalgia helped me to forget the journey back down through the nightmare roads, the sheer cliffs falling away in front of us.

On the *Grand Tour*, we began our trip by travelling from Johannesburg, South Africa's largest city, a huge sprawling place that reminded me of Los Angeles, and which is home to almost nine million people in the greater urban area – much more than I'd thought. It's the economic centre of the region and even though Johannesburg once had a reputation as a dangerous place, it is rapidly regenerating, with trendy cafés moving into formerly no-go areas and the centre, once rife with crime and poverty, now being gradually transformed by art and culture. We visited one of these regenerated areas, Maboneng, and loved the galleries and clothes shops as well as the excellent coffee. There's a place that serves Ethiopian coffee with great ceremony there, and the weekend food market is terrific. However, I'm told that the gap between rich and poor in Johannesburg is still huge – half of the city's residents live in Soweto or its surroundings, while others live in gated communities with high security. In fact, you'll see private security guards as well as the police force, because the relatively high crime rate means that they are needed. I was a bit worried to see signs on the way from the airport warning us about carjackings and not to stop, as they didn't exactly reassure – but gang-related violence, rather than tourist-related, forms a large part of the crime picture in South Africa and sadly affects young men more than anyone else.

Soweto is a city now, home to 1.3 million people and, having grown from a place to which the black population was forced to a city in its own right, it has a culture all of its own. Vilakazi Street is the hub of Soweto and we visited both Archbishop Tutu's and Nelson Mandela's homes, which are both on the same street, and the Soweto Theatre is a fantastic place, but we were told that the 'real' townships on the edge of Soweto were too dangerous to visit. The Apartheid Museum was a really powerful experience and one I won't forget. If you were black in South Africa, you needed to carry a 'pass book' at all times and you weren't allowed to stay in white areas for any length of time without proof that you were there for a reason, for example to work for a white employer. Some of the younger members of our group were only just born when apartheid ended, in 1994, so it was very powerful to stand in a queue at the museum and be allocated a 'white' or 'non-white' entrance to the museum: it really brought it home to us all. We were also very moved by our trip to Robben Island later on, which is where Nelson Mandela was imprisoned for all those years.

From Johannesburg, we flew to the city of East London on the South African coast, then on to the little town of Kenton-on-Sea, which is a tourist resort a bit like Ballybunion, and from there we took a boat ride of 11 kilometres up the Kariega river to Sibuya Game Reserve. The only way in is by boat and we were hopeful that we'd see the 'big five' wild animals: elephant, rhino, Cape buffalo, leopard and lion. They are called the 'big five' because they are the animals most prized by hunters, and before you get yourself in a state, big-game hunting is a major source of income in South Africa. Hunters will spend up to $10,000 on a game-hunting trip. While many feel that no animal should be hunted and killed for sport, others point to the big profits that can be made from legal game hunting, and the amount of jobs it generates – and they also say that because they are stocking private land with wildlife and then breeding them, they are increasing the number of animals, rather than the other way around. Many also say that poaching is the real problem, rather than controlled hunting. The debate will rage on, I'm sure, but South Africans largely accept big-game farming and auctions are as common as our marts are here. Some prized animals can fetch a fortune – in fact, I read one report of an antelope fetching €1.76 million in 2015 because she had really long horns.

Also, game meat is a big thing in South Africa, but you can imagine what yours truly made of it. We paid a visit one night to the aptly named Carnivore Restaurant in Johannesburg, where we were able to eat zebra, ostrich, impala and crocodile, charcoal grilled. You sit at a table with a flag on it and eat until you can eat no more, at which point you lower the flag! It's no place for vegetarians, but they do offer veg – cut into animal shapes ... We saw four of the big five, all except the leopard, during an evening bush drive, so that was a result, and I was delighted the gang managed to see so much.

In Sibuya, I was staying in the owner's house, because there were so many of us. He lived in a permanent tent, and it was nice to live under canvas, albeit with windows and a wood-burning stove. It's an eco-resort, so all electric light is generated by solar power – not great at 3.15 a.m., but otherwise perfect. I was adopted by two frisky kittens that lived outside but who liked to sneak in whenever the tent was left open, jumping up on my bed. When I was getting ready for the early-morning bush drive with my producer, having a very early breakfast, one of my little friends jumped up in my lap, digging his claws into me. My cup of tea flew up into the air and we both were overcome with a fit of the giggles.

Walking with cheetahs was an iconic moment on our trip and we did so at the Tenikwa wildlife refuge. This organisation rescues and rehabilitates wild animals, before returning them to their natural habitat, except for those that can't survive in the wild, which remain in the park. The refuge is a charity and survives on conservation tours and on carefully supervised activities like the cheetah walk. I have done many things on my travels, but seeing a cheetah just saunter past me, ignoring me completely, was an unforgettable experience. I couldn't believe that they didn't see us as 'dinner', but cheetahs are very lazy, apparently: they only chase animals when they are hungry, and they'd been fed – lucky us! We also learned some interesting bush survival skills, including squeezing elephant poo for water. I'm not joking: elephant poo contains a huge amount of water and if you are lost in the bush and come across some, you can give it a good squeeze to extract the water. You'd do it if you had no other choice!

Another highlight of the trip was tagging sharks as part of a shark conservation project that allows people to come along to observe its work. They are trying to persuade people that sharks aren't just the predators we hear about in the headlines, but play a real part in the ecosystem of the sea. The workers spend a lot of time tagging the various species of shark, as well as studying rays and cetaceans – that's whales and dolphins to you and me. These eco-tourism projects are an increasing part of nature tourism and we were delighted to be doing our bit, not to mention getting the chance to see blue sharks up close during a tagging expedition.

Wildlife of a different sort was provided by Ronnie's Sex Shop, which was on the way to our final stop of the tour, Cape Town. In spite of the name, it is not a sex shop! The story goes that Ronnie bought a farm in the early 1980s and wanted to open a little farm shop to sell fresh produce, hence 'Ronnie's Shop', which he painted on the back wall in big letters so everyone could see it. However, while Ronnie was out one day, some of the local boyos decided to add to the description with a bit of graffiti and 'Ronnie's Sex Shop' was born. It wasn't all bad, though, as Ronnie applied for a liquor licence to accommodate all of the sudden visitors and a successful business was born. Now, when you visit, the idea is that you remove an item of underwear and Ronnie will pin it to the bar: there are now hundreds of bras and pairs of underpants hanging from the ceiling – it's some sight! Some of the gang had brought undies from Primark in Belfast – four frilly pairs for the ladies and three pairs of men's briefs. They went in and hung them up in the bar, to find that there were a pair of underpants left over, so they hung them on the back of my seat on the bus. Very funny, I thought, taking them off and going to the back of the bus to return them. 'Here,' I said, 'You can get a refund for these when you get home.'

'Oh, no,' she says, 'they came as part of a three pack!'

Less appealing was Ronnie's 'cuddle puddle' – a room where you can hug others in a non-sexual way. I'm a great man for a hug when it's needed, but not with random strangers.

I was dying to see Cape Town, as I haven't spent a lot of time there and people who have tell me it's fantastic. It has been in the news recently because of the severe drought that the city is enduring at the moment. Due to El Niño, there were three years in a row of drought, and in spite of the rain that did eventually fall, 'day zero' – a day in which there would be no water left and the pipes would be turned off – was due to fall in 2019. Experts have been scrambling to find a solution to Cape Town's water-shortage problems; recent suggestions include having icebergs towed from Antarctica by a marine salvage company to melt down for water. I couldn't help wondering what would happen when the icebergs ran out.

Part of Cape Town's water shortages are caused by tourists, we were told, because up to ten million of them visit the city every year. Ten million! It's hardly surprising as Cape Town has the most spectacular setting, with Table Mountain behind it and the Atlantic Ocean in front. Its setting means that it has always been the focus of foreign attention, first from the Dutch, who used it as a stopping-off point between Europe and Asia, then from the British; because it was also in the middle of all kinds of trading routes, it has been influenced by different cultures. It was also a place to which slaves were sent from Java and other parts of Indonesia, as well as many from Madagascar. These people brought Islam to the Cape as well as their music and food. Today, Cape Malay food is alive and well: big spicy stews like *bredie*, a tomato stew, and *bobotie*, which is considered a really South African dish, and is a cross between lasagne and shepherd's pie, I suppose. I thought it was very tasty. In fact, we had a taste of Cape Malay cuisine during a trip to a home in Bo-Kaap, which is where the Cape Malay community is focused. You might have seen the little houses on travel shows, because they are painted in fizzy-sherbet pinks, greens and yellows.

Cape Town's Langa township is one of the oldest in the country. When we visited it was a Sunday. We walked down a street that was entirely deserted, because no-one in South Africa works on a Sunday. I'm a great believer in that myself, because I don't think it's right to work every day. I'd prefer everyone be off and to have a real sense of a boundary between work and leisure. Today, we're all 'always on', aren't we?

We stumbled across a church during our trip and decided to take a peek in. Once more, I was reminded so much of Ireland, with the men clustered around the front door and all of the women inside. The service was beautiful, with bible readings and South African hymns. All the ladies were in a row with their good shoes on, tapping away to the music, and I had to admire their 'rig-out', as a friend of mine calls it. The ladies all wear nurses' white uniforms and chef's hats, with a bright blue sash, which all looks spotless and very elegant. Some people on the tour got emotional and I don't blame them – the singing and the devotion were so moving.

Outside the front door, a lady had set up her beer stand – I don't think it was a deliberate post-Church experience; it just happened to be nearby! – and she was selling five-litre containers of it for 20c each. Not a lot of money. She had a mountain of old window frames and doors to use as firewood and she was boiling a barrel of water mixed with wheat to make a mash. Can you imagine, keeping three big cauldrons of water on the boil all day? I really admired her dedication.

We were also lucky enough to meet a man on that trip who showed us around his house, which was all made from recycled materials. He was known to everyone in the area as Morgan Freeman, due to his resemblance to the actor, I suppose. He was a retired policeman who had come to Langa township from the Eastern Cape and moved into a little wooden house. He lost everything when the house went on fire in 2013 and vowed never to use wood again, so he'd found an old shipping container and used that instead. He proudly showed us around his container home, which he'd converted into a two-bedroom, kitchen-diner property and I was lost in admiration. Everything – and I mean everything – had been salvaged, from the kitchen tables and chairs to the cooker and a most impressive little table light made out of an old Nutribullet, with a light bulb instead of a chopping blade. It was a real eye-opener and we were very grateful that he let us look around and see what he'd achieved.

That visit with 'Morgan Freeman' sums up everything that I've learned about Africa, as a place where people will make something out of nothing and won't get in a fuss if the world isn't the way they'd like it. They just get on with it and, even though life can be difficult, they never complain. That lady making the beer would make a tiny amount of money and yet she just worked at it, day after day, because it was her job; 'Morgan Freeman' built an entire home out of what he could find and was justly proud of it. It's a lesson I haven't forgotten since: that life is about acceptance and making the most of whatever you have. I think that's what my travels all over the world have taught me: that everyone has challenges in life and overcoming them can be difficult, but never impossible. I have also learned that while countries and cultures may change, people are basically the same the world over.

Reading over my diaries and recalling my travels has made me remember and be grateful for all of the opportunities life has given me, and has helped me to understand how lucky I am to have experienced all of this and to be able to come home to Kerry and reflect on it all. I came across this quote from Chinese writer Lin Yutang: 'No-one realises how beautiful it is to travel until he comes home and rests his head on his old, familiar pillow.' That's certainly true. There's nothing I like better than resting my head on my own pillow in my own bed, no matter how far away I've been. Home is where the heart is, after all, as the writer George Moore said: 'A man travels the world over in search of what he needs and returns home to find it.'

POSTSCRIPT: Route 66

'Nothing behind me,
everything ahead of me,
as is ever so on the road.'

Jack Kerouac

As I write, I have only just returned from the trip of a lifetime, driving the legendary Route 66 in an RV motorhome. I have read about this iconic road many times, and of course I remember the famous Nat King Cole song '(Get Your Kicks on) Route 66'. The song was written by a man called Bobby Troup, who packed his car and headed west along the famous route to make his name in Hollywood, just as so many had before him. As you can imagine, I was absolutely delighted when my nieces and nephews gave me a present of this trip, because, in spite of all my travelling, I was dying to get a sense of the real America, driving west to the Pacific Ocean.

Built in 1926, this road became known as America's Main Street or the Mother Road and is 3,940 kilometres in length, running from Chicago through the state of Illinois, Missouri, Kansas, Oklahoma, Texas, New Mexico, Arizona and finally into California, where the route ends on Santa Monica pier on the shores of the Pacific. Along the way, it throws up a variety of landscapes, from the flat plains of the mid-west, to the desert landscapes of Flagstaff and curious town names like Cuba, Lebanon, Chelsea, Yukon, Clinton, Groom, Vega, Grants, Scallop, Winslow, Essex, Barstow and Beverley Hills until finally, the vast Pacific opens up in front of you.

I could write a whole book on the trip, but for the purposes of this little essay, I'm going to offer just a few highlights of my own three weeks spent on the road: they may not always feature on other people's itineraries, but I think that they offer a real flavour of this all-American experience, with a few little diversions to visit places of interest along the way.

I began in Chicago, Illinois, where I and my travelling companion, Frank, picked up our RV, and had a good nose around its roomy interior. It was very spacious with two double-bed sized bunks, one behind the driving seats and one that pulled out of a little shelf above them. It also had all mod cons, from a cooker and fridge to ample storage space for me to store the bright orange camping pots and pans that one of my nieces had given me for the trip! Now, I feel that I should add here that while the RV is a classic and comfortable way to drive Route 66, it certainly isn't the cheapest. RVs *eat* petrol – the Americans don't do diesel or any biofuels – and we found that a day's driving cost a pricey $160 dollars. Our RV was part of the package, but I think that if you're doing it yourself and are in a little group, car hire and motels might well be cheaper.

Chicago is the Windy City, of course, famous for its skyscrapers, like the John Hancock Tower, and its blues and jazz music, made famous by artists such as Muddy Waters. It's also a great place to shop due to the Magnificent Mile, which is exactly what it says on the tin, a mile-long strip of shops, offering everything from bargain-basement to designer labels. Being a tourist in Chicago offers huge choice, but my top tip would be to get a day pass for their famous water-taxi system. It costs $9 and this allows you to hop on and off at various stages to visit Chinatown, Michigan Avenue and the La Salle district, the historic heart of the city with every architectural style of building represented. You can pick up a map at any Wendella kiosk and it will show you all of the buildings you'll see as you pass by on the river. Chicago also boasts some great food. According to NBC Chicago, the cheeseburger in Au Cheval was voted the number 1 burger in the country for 2018.

Heading south from Chicago sees you on the start of the Route and Springfield, Illinois, the state capital – be aware, there is a Springfield, Missouri too. Springfield is one of those names, like Dublin or indeed Washington, of which there are 88 in the United States! My trip to Springfield reminded me of the time I got two Greensboros confused a few years ago, and ended up in the wrong one, with interesting consequences. I'll make a little diversion here before continuing!

It began with an American guest of ours at the Park Hotel, Kenmare. He had a home on an island in Georgia, called St Simons Island, a big sprawling US-style compound much like the Kennedys' place in Hyannis Port. This man was keen to become a member of the Relais and Châteaux hotel group and he kept asking me to come along and have a look to see if it might make the grade. His home was magnificent, but it was a really rustic family place, so I told him that he could 'remodel' it, as the Americans say, but that it would cost him a lot of money.

Afterwards, I drove from picturesque Savannah up to Charleston and I was flying out of Greensboro, North Carolina, or at least, I thought I was. Now, note that there is also a Greensboro in Vermont, in Pennsylvania, in Alabama. You get the picture! Anyway, in I went to the airport, expecting a tiny regional building, but instead, it looked quite big. I thought that there were an awful lot of people for a small airport, but up I went to the check-in desk anyway. The man at the desk tapped away for a minute or two and then he said, 'I don't see any sign of your booking here.'

After a few more taps, he got to the root of the problem. I had booked a ticket for a Greensboro 700 miles away! I said incredulously, 'Are there two Greensboros?'

'Oh, yes', he replied, 'It happens all the time.'

I now know that there is a grand total of eight Greensboros in the USA, but it was no help to me then, as I had no ticket booked for the actual Greensboro I wanted. 'You'll have to go on standby,' the man said to me.

'Fine,' I sighed. I had to go and sort out my car-hire paperwork, so I went off to do that, then waited in hope for a flight from Greensboro to JFK in New York, then onto Dublin. Of course, the flight was full: it turned out that because this is golf country, half of New York had come down for the weekend to play and were all on their way home. I waited and waited until the man at the check-in desk shouted, 'Quick, go to Gate 14'. Gate 14 was a direct flight to Atlanta, then on to Dublin, which was terrific, but as I went to dash off, I said, 'What about my bags?' Just to add to the confusion, my bags were now on the New York flight!

I was told that my bags would be sent to New York, then over to Shannon and, sure enough, I went home to the hotel and the next day, there was my bag and my suit carrier. I thought, what good service, but when I opened the case, half the things I had packed were gone. And when I opened the suit carrier, my four suits were now two: the jacket from one suit and the pants from another were gone. It would seem that when the bag came to New York, it would have arrived in La Guardia for domestic flights and been taxied to JFK and then to Shannon – and someone decided to have a look and to pick out the best bits. I'm not very tall, and I can imagine that most people in the market for taking things are much taller than me, so I think that I was the inventor of capri pants! The moral of the story is, watch your airport – don't take the first Greensboro you see ...

Just north of Springfield, Illinois lies Funks Grove, the next stop for Frank and myself. It's the home of Funks Grove Maple Sirup, but it's also of great interest to Irish visitors, because of the Celtic cross built there to commemorate a group of Irish emigrants. The monument is in a lovely wooded area and its inscription tells you that these 'more than fifty souls' helped to build the Chicago and Alton Railroad, 'far from the old homes of their hearts, yet forever short of the new homes of their hopes'. The story goes that when these men died (and I'm assuming they would have been men, given their jobs) the bodies of these poor souls were simply piled up by the rail tracks as no-one would take charge of burying them. That is, until a local farmer of German ancestry by the name of Funk Stubblefield offered to bury them in a mass grave on his own farm, which later became a cemetery. I learned that the Funks were no ordinary farming family, but one of the wealthiest in Illinois and Isaac Funk was a friend of none other than Abraham Lincoln.

The Irish emigrant story came to people's attention in the late 1980s and the McLean County Historical Society researched it and decided that it was time to commemorate the event with the fine inscription. While we were there admiring the monument, a lovely lady came up to us, asking if we were Irish. 'It's so nice to see Irish people come by,' she said, 'Because they'd never be remembered otherwise.' I found it very moving to think of these 50 souls, some of whom might be my ancestors or yours, travelling over the Atlantic to the mid-west, in search of a new life, only to die there. We were very moved by it.

Travelling south of Funk's Grove, you come to St Louis, Missouri, on the banks of the great Mississippi River, with all of the history that city offers. I was delighted to visit it because of my old friend, Shirley Dooley, whose funeral I had tried too hard to attend, and was warmly welcomed by her daughter, Peggy and son-in-law, Tony. In St Louis, be sure to visit the Gateway Arch, built to commemorate the great push westwards in the 19th century, even if only to experience the unbelievable lift system to get you to the top. It's brilliant, as you might expect a lift in an arch to be! You sit into a kind of pod, your knees touching your fellow passengers, and this pod zig-zags up the arch, like the steps of stairs, until it reaches the top. A wonder of engineering.

This area has undergone a huge regeneration, with the road being dropped to run below ground and a lovely new park being built in time for the 4 July 2018 celebrations. We also visited Ted Drewes famous frozen custard shop, which is legendary, with a huge queue outside. You can't call it ice-cream though, even if I couldn't tell the difference, or Ted goes mad! Whatever it was, it was delicious, and I got a Ted Drewes T-shirt as a souvenir.

On to Branson, Missouri we drove. It has to be seen to be believed! It's a resort town in the Ozarks, a picturesque area of forest and lakes that stretches across Missouri, Oklahoma and Arkansas. My friend Frank declared Branson to be 'like Bray on steroids'! I mean this in a good way, that it's a mixture of entertainment and pizazz. This resort grew out of humble beginnings when the singer Andy Williams, of 'Moon River' fame, got tired of touring and decided he wanted to find a place where he could perform year-round. For some reason, he picked Branson, this little town in Missouri and built a theatre there, aptly called the Moon River Theatre. It quickly became a destination spot and the highlight of Andy Williams' performing year was his famous Christmas special, broadcast live from Branson. I suppose it'd be a bit like the Rose of Tralee mixed with the Eurovision Song Contest – huge. Nowadays, Branson is home to over 50 theatres with the likes of The Osmonds, Tony Orlando and Dionne Warwick performing regularly. We even saw billboards advertising Nathan Carter and Daniel O'Donnell! They come for a month each and fill a theatre of 600 seats twice or three times a day – I was told that they are very popular because of their clean-cut image. There are no punk rockers in Branson! There are also shows with a religious format, like the epic *Samson*, a story to delight residents of the Christian heartland of America.

Frank and I wondered where the huge crowds thronging this isolated spot came from and we learned that the whole town was built on the premise of 'build it and they will come.' Promoters visit homes for the elderly and clubs around the States and thousands of people are bussed in from all over the place to this little century-old town, which, thanks to some clever marketing and promotion, has become a place that attracts over seven million visitors a year. Visitors will often attend three shows a day, with performances at 14.30 p.m., 17.00 p.m. and 19.30 p.m., and even though they can hardly remember what show is what with all of the excitement, they all seemed to be having a good time!

Frank and I went to see Clay Cooper, a country-and-western singer, just to say that we'd taken in a show and he was actually very good. He had some great stage banter, Joe Dolan style – at one point, he asked the audience if they needed some refreshments and someone piped up, 'A Bud Light!' Well, there was audible gasp from this conservative audience, as this is not a drinking place. Clay Cooper gave out to the poor man, but when the second half opened, true to his word, Clay said, 'I have a surprise' and he produced two cans of Bud Light. 'I ran out to the garage at half-time and got them for you.' He probably had, or someone had anyway, because there was absolutely no bar in the theatre. Clay Cooper is a married man in his 50s, and his wife is a dancer and his two children also perform in the show, so it's very much family fun. It has to be said, there was a touch of the school concert about the whole thing, but I found it highly entertaining.

Our next stop was Oklahoma, a nice mid-western city that has sadly become best-known for the terrible bombing that happened there in 1995, by the anti-government terrorist Timothy McVeigh, when 168 people were killed, including many young children. There is a very moving monument to those who lost their lives at the spot where the bombing occurred, a park full of sculpted empty chairs going from big to small, one for every person who died. The museum is also a must-visit, as it tells the story in a straightforward and engaging way right until the execution of McVeigh. A really moving place.

On a happier note, Oklahoma is also the home of the Will Rogers Memorial Rodeo in Vinita. Known as the Cowboy Philosopher, Will Rogers was once one of America's biggest movie stars, one of the heroes of the Vaudeville years. This actor of Cherokee stock is remembered fondly in Oklahoma, not least because of his many funny quotes. One of my favourites is, 'I don't make jokes. I just watch the government and report the facts,' which has a certain resonance these days! I also think that this saying of his is very apt: 'Do the best that you can, and don't take life too serious.' True.

Gas stations and diners are scattered all along Route 66, many restored to their 1950's glory, with Coke machines and their original gas pumps, which really add atmosphere to the drive, even if some of the old route actually runs alongside the new interstate, which surprised me a little. However, there is still a lot of genuine Route 66 to be seen, from motels, many with their original signs 'out front' and truck stops to bridges, such as the famous William H. Murray bridge, near Bridgeport, Oklahoma. It's a prime example of a 'pony truss' for you bridge enthusiasts and its 38 truss arches are very impressive as you drive over the South Canadian river.

As you go through Oklahoma towards Texas, you wander in and out of Native American territories, and road signs tell you that you are entering Cherokee or Muskogee or Cheyenne lands. In fact, there are 39 tribes in this part of the route. A look at the very helpful www.americanindiansandroute66.com informed me that Oklahoma is a combination of two Choctaw words: 'ukla' = person and 'huma' = red. I also learned about famous Native Americans such as Will Rogers, but also a man called Andrew Hartley Payne, a Cherokee who won the inaugural 3,400-mile road race to celebrate the opening of Route 66. He won $25,000, which must have been an enormous sum at the time and, like a good son, he paid off his parents' mortgage with the proceeds.

Amarillo, Texas was our next stop, known as the home of the largest wind farms in the country, but also home to the biggest steak house, The Big Texan Steak Ranch. Built on Route 66 by a man called Bob Lee in the 1960s, it soon became an iconic stopping-off point for travellers, and the sign, held by a giant cowboy, became famous. Bob Lee was clearly a canny man, because when Route 66 was replaced by the new interstate in the 1970s, he had a bigger restaurant built beside the motorway and moved the cowboy up there for good measure. He was obviously a born entrepreneur.

Our RV stop was a short drive from the Ranch, and they sent a huge limo bedecked in steer horns to bring us there! The driver told me that they take up to 600 people a day to the restaurant in limos like this. Imagine if we ferried everyone to the Park Hotel, Kenmare in a limo! If we did, our guests might well get notions ... Frank and I had a great time, and our journey reminded me of another limo trip, this time in Las Vegas. Bear with me!

It was millennium year, and we had a big budget for the staff holiday, so we decided we'd really push the boat out and go to Las Vegas. I had arranged a coach transfer for us from the airport to our hotel, but I'd also booked a big white stretch limo for four of the staff, and would draw names from a hat on the way over. I made it simple by tearing up lots of little bits of white paper, and then adding four little bits of blue paper to the hat, asking everyone to take their pick, but not telling them what they'd won until they got to Las Vegas, where the coach was waiting. And beside the coach was a giant of a stretch limo in the brightest of white, complete with tinted windows and a sliding sunroof.

'Who has the blue bits of paper?' I asked. 'Come on up here and claim your prize.' I can still remember that Mary and Joan who work in accommodation were two winners, so I opened the door of the limo and said, 'Hop in.'

Joan thought I was pulling her leg, so she said, 'I'm not getting in.' I said, 'Joan, you are to get in. I'm not messing. It really is for you.' Eventually, we persuaded the four winners to climb on board and took lots of photos of them waving to the rest of us, like royalty. A little while later, we were rumbling up the strip in our bus, when the limo pulled up alongside us, the roof slid back and the four were inside with their champagne!

Meanwhile, back on the ranch ... the numbers in the Big Texan are staggering, and indeed when we got there, it was full to bursting with people eating their steaks. It was a big barn of a place with cow-hide tablecloths and a large galleried area where you could look down on the main event, the 72oz-steak-eating contest. Three contestants sit up on a raised platform underneath three timers and they have 60 minutes to eat a 72oz steak, with the winner getting their steak for free. An hour to eat a steak might seem like a long time, but it's four and a half pounds we're talking about here, or two kilos, so that's a lot of steak! The all-time champion of the event is a 120lb girl who ate hers in 4 minutes and downed another one in 5 minutes. I don't know what kind of a gut she had if she could digest all of that. My favourite bit of the evening, however, was being serenaded by two ancient cowboys. They informed us that they had once been a trio, but one of them had passed on. The older of the two had a giant double bass, bigger than himself, and they gamely belted out a country-and-western standard. It all added to the atmosphere!

Amarillo is also home to a rather strange attraction, the Cadillac Museum, which consists of a row of Cadillac cars, half-buried in an open field, which you can decorate with spray paint. It's an art form of a kind, I suppose, and I did make my mark on it, even if I thought 'only in America' while doing so!

New Mexico, the next state on our drive, has some lovely all-American diners and motels, such as the Blue Swallow in Tucumcari, which still proudly displays the original road sign, as well as bedrooms with vintage furnishings and my favourite, the El Rancho, in Gallup, which has the most fantastic façade, with Greek columns and a huge pink neon surround. It was originally a film location, so many of Hollywood's finest, from Kirk Douglas to Katharine Hepburn, Spencer Tracy, even Ronald Reagan, stayed there, and the lofty interior, with its dark wood, is a sight to behold.

Bard, New Mexico, is best known for Russell's Travel Center, a diner and truckstop, which also has a car museum, and you don't have to be a car nut to enjoy it. I certainly admired the huge Cadillacs, Corvettes and Chevrolets with their fold-out trays for your popcorn at the drive-in, or the roof that slides back under the trunk of the car. They are testament to the American love of the car and also to a time and a place when America did everything bigger and better – it truly ruled the world and on Route 66, you can see just how.

New Mexico is where the desert landscape really unfolds and as we drove on to Arizona, rock formations and mountains began to appear, which reminded me of all the cowboy movies I'd watched as a child. I could just see Gary Cooper standing there, guns at the ready! The nature in Arizona is unbelievable. Of course, there's the Grand Canyon, which was a bit far north for us to visit this time, as was Monument Valley, the backdrop to many a cowboy movie, but Painted Desert and the Petrified Forest National Park, were new discoveries. Painted Desert has remarkable colours in its layers of rock, laid down over millions of years and the Petrified Forest, with its thousands of fallen trees filled with a myriad of colours felt like something from a science-fiction novel. Our guide told us that over 200 million years ago the forest was buried in volcanic ash, then slowly the wood was embalmed with silica and then in essence became stone. Nature is unbelievable. We also went to the site of a huge meteor crater, near Scottsdale, one mile wide and four miles in circumference, which apparently is very recent in geological terms at a mere 50,000 years old! All I can remember is that it was absolutely baking and watching in astonishment as a group took a tour down into the crater – they'd boil alive, I thought.

One little side trip took us to Sedona, Arizona, and if you want spectacular mountain vistas, then this is the place for you. I drove Frank mad with all the ooh-ing and ahh-ing over the scenery! Sedona is lovely, but you'll need plenty of money, as this is the most expensive stop on the trip. I paid for a smoothie and a two-scoop cone there and the server said, 'that'll be twenty-one dollars and eighty-five cents please.' For a smoothie and an ice-cream! My advice would be to enjoy looking around, but keep your money in your pocket. Sedona has a big New Age movement in it and offers lots of spiritual courses for those – with money! - who are into soul-searching.

We then travelled over the mountain to Oatman, Arizona, another cowboy town, but with a simpler feel than that of chichi Sedona. It made its mark as a producer of large quantities of gold, but those years are long gone and after falling into decline, it is now a real-life, Wild West town. It feels very authentic, with the little clapboard houses and wooden store fronts, and people wear vintage clothing, clearly dressing the part! They have a number of daily 'shoot-outs' on the main street, which are highly entertaining.

Oatman is also famous as the honeymoon location of Clark Gable and Carole Lombard, two of the stars of Hollywood's Golden Age, who spent the first night of their honeymoon in the Oatman Hotel. The room is perfectly preserved, including the tiny bed – they really were much smaller in those days, unless one of them slept on the floor! Today, the town is also famous for its many wild donkeys or *burros*, as they are also called. These donkeys were left behind after the goldmines closed and they took up residence in the town, wandering the streets and being fed by the locals and by visitors. You can buy special packs of food which have been prepared for donkey diets to feed them, and they all look very healthy on it.

Lake Havasu City, our next stop, was a very modern town, which grew up in the spot where a local entrepreneur recreated London Bridge, having imported an actual bridge from London that had once crossed the River Thames. This man, Robert P. McCulloch, bought the bridge and had it moved, lock, stock, and barrel to this spot in Arizona. Lake Havasu City is also a hot spot for the famous, or infamous, Spring Break, when the students get their holidays in America. They all flock to this town and London Bridge itself is a huge tourist draw. I have to say, I found the bridge to be very impressive, but a bit out of place in this setting, surrounded by tacky 'English pubs' and tearooms. A touch of Vegas here, I think! A final interesting stop in Arizona was a place called Winslow, which was immortalised in the Eagles song 'Take it Easy'. They haven't been slow to capitalise on the connection and you can have your photo taken in the exact same spot as songwriters Glenn Frey and Jackson Browne.

When we reached Carson, California, we returned our RV and rented a car to head to San Diego for two nights. My companion's brother, Joe Dowling of Abbey Theatre fame, was opening *The Tempest* as guest director for the Old Globe Shakespeare theatre summer season. I was unsure of my interest in Shakespeare but was delighted to be there for the opening night.

As we deposited our RV in Carson, all that was left on the bed were two $8 blankets which we bought on day one in Chicago in case they were needed. Indeed they were, but to shield us from the terrific AC unit in the RV! I tossed them into the boot of the car for someone in need, should we see anyone sleeping out overnight. We met Joe and his wife Siobhan for dinner that evening and discussed his project and our trip. He had kindly arranged tickets for us, and as the theatre is an outdoor amphitheatre style, warned us to wear a jacket as it gets very cold when the sun goes down. In fact, he says they even rent blankets to patrons. When we came back to our hotel that night I thought of our blankets in the boot and moved them into the car so as not to forget them on opening night. Next evening we headed off for an early dinner and the show. Joe had a programme for each of us which detailed the cast and a show synopsis. I noted the pages of wealthy theatre donors, the top donor being in the $25 million per year category! Anyway, undeterred we took our seats about four rows back. I was having a great time trying to decide which guest gave the $25 million!

As the show progressed, I was trying to keep up with the story as the names alone were hard to follow – Gonzalo, Trinculo and Sycorax. Then I suddenly realised I was freezing! Out came the $8 blankets to be shared by all, much to our delight and theirs. The show was terrific after that and I really enjoyed Joe's excellent production. When the play was over, I carefully folded the blankets and said to Joe that, as we were heading back to Ireland in the morning, we would 'donate' the two blankets to the Old Globe on the condition that our donation would appear amongst the donors listed in the programme – even if it appeared below the $25 million category. We await next year's publication!

After all our wanderings, we finally reached the end of the road at Santa Monica pier. I had been there many times but after a journey of 4,000 kilometres, including our little diversions from the main route, this was a special homecoming. The pier is so vibrant with the big Ferris wheel, guys doing three-card tricks, juggling, fire-eating and the throngs of people from all over the world, all enjoying the Californian sunshine, it was a really celebratory welcome, Frank and I had our picture taken in front of the iconic Route 66 sign and took in the ambiance of the place, while we remembered the highlights of our epic journey. I spend a lot of my time in aeroplanes, but there truly is nothing like zipping along, the wind in your hair, the road stretching in front of you. I can see why it appealed, and continues to appeal, to so many Americans. It really embodies the spirit of the country, that sense of hopefulness and a brighter future, and, of course, the freedom of the open road. An unforgettable journey.